KiDS
in the kitchen

THE AUSTRALIAN
Women's Weekly

KiDS
in the kitchen

acp
books

contents

gettingstarted

We all have to eat and, eventually, you'll probably have to cook to feed yourself. Now, when you have the family kitchen and a helpful adult around 24/7, is the perfect time to learn about food and how to cook. We bet it won't take long for you to discover that cooking is a lot more than just making food to eat: it's heaps of fun, and creative and exciting, too.

Here are some basic tips for getting it right in the kitchen: even your mum and dad and professional chefs stick to simple safety and hygiene guidelines like these.

Before you start

Make sure you've got the okay from an adult to use the kitchen before you start anything, and ask someone to hang around the first few times you make something. Even professional cooks don't know everything, and they all have assistants, so never be afraid to ask an adult to explain a recipe to you or for help in doing something.

Understand the recipe

Read the recipe through a few times before you start preparing. Make sure you know when you have to start cooking, what ingredients and utensils you need, and if something in the menu needs to be made a day ahead.

Defrosting meat

Always thaw meat, seafood and poultry, covered, in the refrigerator. In a pinch, you can defrost these items in your microwave oven, but take care because some outside edges of the meat can actually cook. Place meat on a tray in the refrigerator as it defrosts to stop it dripping onto other food.

Keep your hair out of the food

Tie long hair back from your face to keep it from falling into the food or onto food preparation surfaces. It will also keep you from singeing any wayward strands. Now you know why most chefs wear hats.

Personal hygiene

Don't touch your hair or mouth, or leave the kitchen to do something else, without washing your hands again before touching any food. Stay out of the kitchen if you're sick.

Clean hands

Always wash your hands with soap and warm water (don't forget your fingernails), and dry them on a clean towel or absorbent paper. This is extremely important when you're handling uncooked food. Before making sandwiches, cutting a fruit salad or tossing salad vegetables, always wash your hands thoroughly. If you have a cut on your hand, wear disposable gloves. Always wash your hands after touching any uncooked meat, seafood or poultry.

Clothing

Wear short-sleeved or tight-fitting long-sleeved tops. Loose-fitting ones can drop into the food, or worse, catch fire over a hot stove.

Watch your feet

Wear closed-toed shoes when cooking (more than one chef has dropped a sharp knife, point-first, onto his or her toes). It's not a bad idea to wear non-slip shoes as well.

Tidy up as you go

Keep the benchtop and the rest of the preparation area clean and tidy as you work. Wipe up any spills or grease spots that occur during cooking as you go. Never use the same cloth for wiping up spills, for your hands or for the kitchen benchtop. Rinse the cloth or sponge you use constantly in hot soapy water. And if you wash any equipment you've used, or at least rinse it well, you can use it again for the next thing you're going to make. Even if you don't use it again, at least the cooked food won't have been able to cement itself to the bottom of the pans while you're eating.

Taste as you go

It's a good idea to taste food as you prepare it, to test for flavour, but don't taste from the stirring spoon or salad fork then return it into the saucepan or serving bowl; use different, clean fresh cutlery every time you taste. And don't add salt to enhance the flavour: your idea of perfect seasoning may be far too much for someone else.

Put stuff away

Put the food you've finished with back in the refrigerator or pantry, checking first to make certain that the lids are on tight. If you're putting away any uncooked meat, seafood or poultry, make sure it's enclosed tightly in plastic wrap or a snap-lock bag, or sealed tightly in a storage container. Ditto with raw vegies: wrap them tightly and return them to the crisper in the fridge.

kitchenequipment

Knives

Choosing the right knife for the right job is something you'll learn over time. Most cooks use only four or five different knives; ask the main cook in your family for advice as well as vital safety tips.

Grater

Used for shredding vegetables, cheese and, if you haven't got a crusher, garlic (using the smallest holes). Take care that you don't grate your knuckles or fingertips on the razor-sharp holes.

Saucepans

Come in many shapes and sizes and, like knives, each pan has a different purpose, capacity being just one. Make sure you turn a pan's handles away from the stove's front to avoid knocking the pan onto the floor.

Whisks

The best tool for beating or whipping air into egg whites or cream, to stiffen or increase them in volume, is a whisk. You'll have to learn how to rotate your wrist to whisk well, but it's not difficult.

Chopping boards

Whether it's plastic or wood, your chopping board must be kept really clean. Try keeping different coloured boards for different foods: red for raw meat; yellow for bread; and green for vegies and fruit.

Measuring spoons

Sold as sets measuring from 1 tablespoon for the largest down to 1/8 teaspoon for the smallest, they measure both dry and liquid ingredients. Level the top flat with the back of a knife for accuracy with dry ingredients.

Measuring cups

These come in sets, too, usually sized to measure 1, 1/2, 1/3 and 1/4 cups. Spoon dry ingredients into the cup then drag the back of a knife across the surface to level the top of the cup's content.

Kitchen scales

For measuring foods (like whole fruits or spaghetti) that can't be squeezed into a measuring cup, or when needing an exact weight for flour or sugar when baking, use your kitchen scales.

Liquid measuring jugs

These have millilitre and cup measurements written down the side. To measure precisely, place the jug on a level surface and pour in an approximate amount of liquid. Face the jug at eye level and check the quantity for accuracy.

Melon baller

You'll find many uses for this tool besides scooping out melon (potato, butter and ice-cream, too) balls: for instance, coring apples and pears, or scraped down the side of chocolate to make long curls.

Electrical appliances

A toaster, kettle or any electrical appliance is easy enough to use, but remember to unplug them when you've finished cooking a meal and before cleaning them. Remember to never leave the kitchen with any electrical appliance operating.

Oven mitts

Oven mitts or pot holders protect your fingers from being burned by escaping steam from a lifted lid or when pouring hot liquid, as well as the obvious — taking hot dishes out of the oven or microwave.

Pastry brushes

Flat wood brushes, with either natural or plastic bristles, are used for greasing oven trays and cake pans; brushing water or milk on the edges of pastry parcels to seal them; or to brush a marinade onto food.

Wooden spoons

A favourite tool of many cooks, wooden spoons are great to stir with because they don't scratch non-stick surfaces and are comfortable in your hand. Make sure to wash and dry thoroughly after use.

Spatulas

These long-handled utensils have flat plastic or rubber, or even wood or metal ends, perfect for scraping cake batter from a bowl or folding whipped or beaten food into a mixture without deflating it.

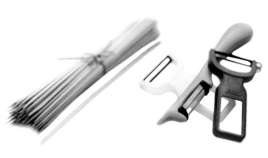   

Skewers

Vegetables, meat, seafood and poultry can be threaded onto skewers for grilling. If you use wooden or bamboo skewers, soak them in water for an hour before using so they don't splinter or scorch.

Vegetable peelers

Not only do these peel potatoes, apples and the like, they also slice carrots, green mango or cucumber into super-fine ribbons for salads, and potato into thin enough slices to fry for homemade chips.

Microplane

The microplane is a new version of a traditional zester. It looks like a small metal cricket bat covered with sharp tiny holes. It can be used to grate rind, chocolate, cheese, garlic or ginger.

Cutters

There are dozens of cutter sizes and designs; use them to cut out biscuits or shapes from rolled-out dough to top a pie. They make good templates to fill with sprinkles or icing sugar on cake tops.

Strainers

These are used to shake sifted dry ingredients like icing sugar over the top of a cake or to drain cooked pasta or vegies. Strain your fresh juice into a glass to capture the pips and pulp.

howdoyoudoit?

Removing bacon rind

When chopping bacon, it's a good idea to cut away the hard outside rind first. Place the rashers on a chopping board; using a sharp knife, cut through fat as close to rind as possible along the length of the rasher. Scissors can also ← be used to do this job neatly.

Chop onions finely

Cut the top end from an onion then slice the onion in half lengthways; discard skin from both halves. Slice each half thinly, first lengthways then widthways. Throw away the onion root end and green core. ➡

Crush and peel garlic

Separate, but do not peel, garlic cloves from the bulb; place on a chopping board then use the flat side of a heavy knife to press down firmly on each clove. As the clove is flattened, the skin splits and will be easy to pull off. Next, crush or chop the garlic according to how you want it.

Prepare capsicums

Hold the capsicum stem in one hand then slice lengthways into quarters with a sharp knife. Discard the stem and seed core. Flatten quarters, skin-side down, on a chopping board; run the knife flat across each piece to remove membrane and ← remaining seeds.

Separate lettuce leaves

With the cored-end facing down, smash lettuce hard onto the bench. This will loosen the outer leaves, which will then come away easily. Holding the cored end under cold running water will also force the outer leaves to fall off intact. ➡

Seed tomatoes

Some recipes, salsa, for example, call for seeded tomatoes, usually so that the final mixture won't be too watery. First, cut the tomato in half lengthways then use a teaspoon to scoop out the seeds and pulp (if you want to keep these for another use, scoop them into a bowl).

⬇

Peel a tomato

Cut a shallow cross in the base of the tomato. Place the tomato in a heatproof bowl; cover with boiling water, stand 2 minutes then cover tomato with cold water to cool. Use your fingers to peel away the skin; starting from the ⬅ cross end, pull towards the top.

Roasting capsicums

Place prepared capsicum quarters, skin-side up, on oven tray under heated grill or in very hot oven until the skin blisters and blackens. Place capsicum pieces in an airtight paper or plastic bag for 10 minutes then ⬅ peel the skin away carefully.

Slice and seed an avocado

Use a small knife to make several lengthways cuts around the avocado, through to the seed. Use your fingers to pull away the strips of peel, from stem-end downward, then use the knife to lever out the slices, one at a time. *To seed an avocado*, cut the avocado in half lengthways around the seed. Twist halves in different directions. Use ⬅ a spoon to scoop out the seed.

how do you do it?

Separating an egg

Crack an egg gently over a small bowl with the back of a knife. Transfer the yolk from half-shell to half-shell until all the white drops into the bowl. Another method is to crack an egg into a small shallow bowl or saucer, cover the yolk with a glass then tilt the saucer carefully so that the white runs into a separate bowl.

Melting chocolate

Break chocolate pieces into a microwave-safe bowl; place in microwave oven on MEDIUM (55%) for 1 minute for every 200g of chocolate. Take the bowl out of the microwave using oven mitts and stir the chocolate. If it hasn't melted completely, repeat the microwave oven melting method, in shorter bursts, until chocolate is smooth.

Juice a lemon

To get as much juice from a lemon as possible, place it in a microwave oven on HIGH (100%) for 30 seconds, or cover it with hot water for about a minute. Next, roll it, pressing firmly, along your kitchen bench, to break up the pulp and release more juice. ➡

Grating lemon rind

Use a citrus zester (or microplane if you have one) or the smallest holes on a four-sided grater. Carefully grate the rind onto a piece of baking paper; it will slide easily off the paper. Don't press down too hard on the lemon because you only want to grate the outer yellow rind. Always grate a lemon before you juice it.

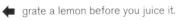

Testing if a cake is done

Push a metal skewer into the highest part of the cake. You can use a wooden one, but it's easier to tell if there's cake mixture stuck on a metal skewer. Pull the skewer out, and if no cake mixture sticks to it, the cake is cooked. ➡

Roasting nuts

Roasting nuts releases their flavour and changes them from soft to crunchy. Spread the quantity of nuts you're using in a single layer onto an oven tray then roast in a preheated moderate oven for about 5 minutes. You can also stir the nuts in a dry frying pan over medium heat until they are lightly browned and fragrant. ⬇

Turn out a cake

Using tea-towels or oven mitts, remove the cake pan from the oven and sit pan on a wooden board. Turn the cake upside-down onto a wire rack; remove pan then the lining paper. Put another rack over cake bottom and, holding the two racks like a sandwich, turn the cake over ⬅ so it now is top-side up.

Cut citrus rind strips

If necessary, ask an adult to help you remove the rind from a lemon, orange or lime; cut away any of the bitter white pith that sticks to the rind. Use a sharp knife to cut the rind into really thin strips to ⬅ sprinkle over salads or desserts.

Make strawberry fans

Make four or five vertical cuts into a strawberry from the tip end, being careful not to cut all the way through. Gently spread the slices into a fan shape to decorate ice-creams or cakes, or to hang over the rim of a ⬅ juice or smoothie glass.

breakfast

PREPARATION TIME 5 MINUTES | COOKING TIME 5 MINUTES | SERVES 4

porridge

ingredients:

3½ cups (875ml) hot water
1½ cups (135g) rolled oats
½ cup (125ml) milk

method:

1 Combine the hot water and rolled oats in medium saucepan; cook, stirring, over medium heat about 5 minutes or until porridge is thick and creamy.
2 Stir in milk. Serve with the topping of your choice.

per serving (without topping)
4.1g total fat (**1.3g** saturated fat); **627kJ** (**150 cal**); **23.4g** carbohydrate; **4.7g** protein; **2.3g** fibre

toppings

CINNAMON SUGAR

Combine 1 teaspoon ground cinnamon with 2 tablespoons caster sugar in small bowl. Sprinkle over bowls of porridge. Any remaining cinnamon sugar can be sprinkled on hot buttered toast for an after-school snack.

per serving (with porridge)
1.6g total fat (**0.6g** saturated fat); **259kJ** (**62 cal**); **9.7g** carbohydrate; **1.9g** protein; **0.7g** fibre

HONEY AND **YOGURT**

Divide ⅓ cup (95g) vanilla yogurt and 1 tablespoon honey among bowls of porridge.

per serving (with porridge)
4.1g total fat (**1.3g** saturated fat); **773kJ** (**185 cal**); **31.4g** carbohydrate; **4.7g** protein; **2.3g** fibre

tip

> **Eating a good breakfast kick-starts your day, helping you to concentrate better in school. It also gives you plenty of the minerals and vitamins you need to keep going all day.**

APPLE AND PEAR **COMPOTE**

Peel, core and coarsely chop 1 large apple and 1 medium pear. Combine fruit with ⅓ cup apple juice and 1 tablespoon lemon juice in medium saucepan over medium heat; bring to a boil. Reduce heat; simmer, covered, stirring occasionally, about 15 minutes or until fruit softens and liquid is absorbed.

per serving (with porridge)
4.2g total fat (**1.3g** saturated fat); **899kJ** (**215 cal**); **37.5g** carbohydrate; **5g** protein; **4.2g** fibre

PREPARATION TIME 5 MINUTES | COOKING TIME 10 MINUTES | SERVES 4

scrambled eggs with **chorizo**

ingredients:

250g chorizo sausages, sliced thickly

8 eggs

¾ cup (180ml) cream

2 tablespoons coarsely chopped fresh chives

10g butter

method:

1 Cook chorizo in medium frying pan until browned and cooked through; cover to keep warm.

2 Break one egg into small bowl, then pour into large jug. Repeat with remaining eggs. When all eggs are in jug, whisk until well combined, then whisk in cream and half of the chives.

3 Melt butter in medium frying pan over low heat, add egg mixture; cook, stirring gently, until egg mixture just begins to set.

4 Serve chorizo and scrambled eggs, sprinkled with remaining chives, on slices of toasted bread of your choice, if desired.

tip

➡ **Eggs are an excellent form of protein: a large one will provide you with about 20 per cent of your recommended daily requirement.**

Slicing sausage diagonally makes the finished dish look more attractive.

Scrambling eggs over low heat keeps them soft and creamy.

didyou know?

Chorizo is a Spanish sausage made with coarsely ground pork and highly seasoned with garlic and chillies. But if you would rather use your favourite kind of sausage instead – no problem.

per serving **45.9g** total fat (**23.1g** saturated fat); **2128kJ** (**509 cal**); **3.7g** carbohydrate; **21.7g** protein; **0.9g** fibre

PREPARATION TIME 10 MINUTES | COOKING TIME 10 MINUTES | SERVES 4

tip

➡ **Break eggs, one at a time, into a small bowl before combining them. This way, if one is bad, you can throw it out without ruining the rest. And by sliding the egg into the baking dish you are less likely to splash or to break the yolk.**

Using a sharp knife, chop the ham coarsely on a chopping board.

Break eggs one at a time into a small bowl before sliding into baking dishes.

◯ baked eggs with ham and cheese

ingredients:

50g shaved ham, chopped coarsely
2 green onions, chopped finely
4 eggs
⅓ cup (40g) coarsely grated cheddar cheese

method:

1 Preheat oven to moderate (180°C/160°C fan-forced). Grease four ½-cup (125ml) ovenproof dishes.
2 Divide ham and onion among dishes. Break one egg into small bowl, then carefully slide egg from bowl over ham and onion in dish. Repeat with remaining eggs. Sprinkle dishes with equal amounts of cheese.
3 Place dishes on oven tray; bake, uncovered, about 10 minutes or until egg yolk is just set.

per serving **9.1g** total fat (**3.9g** saturated fat); **539kJ** (**129 cal**); **0.4g** carbohydrate; **11.6g** protein; **0.1g** fibre

21

PREPARATION TIME 15 MINUTES | COOKING TIME 10 MINUTES | SERVES 4

○ waffles with maple syrup and **strawberries**

ingredients:
8 packaged Belgian-style waffles (400g)
20g butter
500g strawberries, hulled, sliced thickly
½ cup (125ml) pure maple syrup

method:
1 Preheat oven to moderately slow (170°C/150°C fan-forced).
2 Place waffles, in single layer, on oven tray; heat, in oven, about 8 minutes.
3 Meanwhile, melt butter in medium frying pan; cook strawberries, stirring gently, about 2 minutes or until just heated through. Add maple syrup; cook, stirring gently, until heated through.
4 Divide waffles among serving plates; top with strawberry maple mixture.

per waffle 22.8g total fat (**10.4g** saturated fat); **2316kJ** (**554 cal**); **73.5g** carbohydrate; **12.4g** protein; **4.9g** fibre

tips

➡ **You can find Belgian-style waffles on supermarket shelves and in most most delicatessens.**
➡ **Pure maple syrup is a rich-tasting, dark-brown syrup made from the sap of maple trees; the syrup that is called maple-flavoured (or pancake syrup) on the label isn't the "real thing" and is not a good substitute.**
➡ **Hulling a strawberry means cutting around the leafy part at the top to remove the green and a bit of the core.**

Stir the strawberries gently so that they hold their shape and don't become mushy.

per pancake **10.7g** total fat (**6.7g** saturated fat);
869kJ (**208 cal**); **23.4g** carbohydrate;
4.4g protein; **0.8g** fibre

PREPARATION TIME 10 MINUTES (PLUS REFRIGERATION TIME) | COOKING TIME 20 MINUTES | MAKES 16

Each pancake should be made using about a quarter cup of the batter.

When lots of bubbles pop up on the surface, turn pancake with a spatula.

buttermilk pancakes with raspberry **butter**

ingredients:

2 cups (300g) self-raising flour
⅓ cup (75g) caster sugar
2 eggs, beaten lightly
600ml buttermilk
50g butter, melted
1 tablespoon finely grated lemon rind
cooking-oil spray
125g butter, softened
¼ cup (80g) raspberry jam

method:

1 Sift flour and sugar into large bowl. Whisk eggs, buttermilk, melted butter and rind in medium bowl. Gradually whisk egg mixture into flour mixture; whisk until mixture makes a smooth batter. Transfer batter to large jug. Cover; refrigerate batter 30 minutes.

2 Lightly spray large heavy-based frying pan with cooking-oil spray. Make 4 pancakes at a time by pouring ¼ cup batter into heated pan for each pancake. Cook pancakes, uncovered, until bubbles appear on surface; turn pancakes over with spatula to lightly brown other side. Place pancakes on plate; cover with foil to keep warm. Make 12 more pancakes, in three more batches, with remaining batter.

3 Beat softened butter in small bowl with electric mixer until light and creamy. Add jam; continue beating until combined.

4 Place pancakes on serving plates; serve topped with raspberry butter.

PREPARATION TIME 15 MINUTES | COOKING TIME 15 MINUTES | MAKES 8

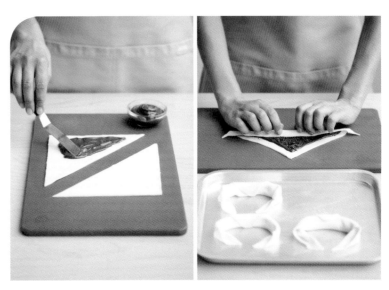

► **Croissants are better eaten warm than at room temperature.**

Spread chocolate-hazelnut spread evenly over each of the triangles, leaving a 1cm border all around.

Roll each triangle, starting at the widest side, to enclose the chocolate-hazelnut spread and chocolate filling.

chocolate hazelnut **croissants**

ingredients:

2 sheets ready-rolled puff pastry
⅓ cup (110g) chocolate-hazelnut spread
30g dark eating chocolate, grated finely
25g butter, melted
1 tablespoon icing sugar

method:

1 Preheat oven to hot (220°C/200°C fan-forced). Lightly grease two oven trays.
2 Cut pastry sheets diagonally to make four triangles. Spread triangles with chocolate-hazelnut spread, leaving a 1cm border; sprinkle each evenly with chocolate.
3 Roll triangles, starting at wide end; curve ends in slightly to form crescent shape. Place 3cm apart on trays; brush croissants with melted butter.
4 Bake, uncovered, about 12 minutes or until croissants are browned lightly and cooked through. Serve croissants lightly dusted with sifted icing sugar.

per croissant 17.7g total fat (**4.8g** saturated fat); **1158kJ**
(**277 cal**); **26.4g** carbohydrate; **3.4g** protein; **0.9g** fibre

mother'sdaybreakfast

PREPARATION TIME 15 MINUTES | COOKING TIME 15 MINUTES | SERVES 4

○ orange and ginger juice

ingredients: 8 medium oranges (2kg)
6cm piece fresh ginger (30g), grated

method: **1** Juice oranges on citrus squeezer; discard seeds. Stir in ginger.
2 Pour into four serving glasses.

per serving **0.4g** total fat (**0g** saturated fat); **589kJ**
(**141 cal**); **27.2g** carbohydrate; **3.7g** protein; **6.8g** fibre

28

PREPARATION TIME 5 MINUTES | COOKING TIME 3 MINUTES | MAKES 4

○ pears on fruit **toast**

ingredients:
4 slices fruit bread
1 small pear (180g), sliced thinly
2 teaspoons brown sugar

method:
1 Preheat grill.
2 Toast fruit bread.
3 Place pear slices on each slice of toast.
4 Sprinkle pear with sugar. Toast under grill about
2 minutes or until browned lightly.

per toast **1.3g** total fat (**0.2g** saturated fat); **518kJ**
(**124 cal**); **25.2g** carbohydrate; **2.8g** protein; **2.4g** fibre

29

PREPARATION TIME 25 MINUTES (PLUS REFRIGERATION TIME) SERVES 4

○ peach bircher **muesli**

ingredients:

2 cups (220g) natural muesli
1⅓ cups (330ml) apple juice
¾ cup (200g) country-style yogurt
1¼ cups (185g) coarsely chopped dried peaches
2 tablespoons honey
¾ cup (180ml) milk
1 large apple (200g), peeled, grated
1 large peach (220g), cut into wedges
¼ cup (20g) toasted shredded coconut

method:

1 Combine muesli, juice, yogurt, dried peach, honey and milk in large bowl. Cover; refrigerate overnight.
2 Stir apple into muesli mixture; serve topped with peach wedges and sprinkled with coconut.

per serving **12g** total fat (**6.6g** saturated fat); **2149kJ** (**514 cal**); **82.4g** carbohydrate; **12.4g** protein; **12.1g** fibre

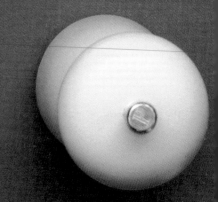

PREPARATION TIME 15 MINUTES | COOKING TIME 15 MINUTES   4

mushroom, capsicum and cheese omelettes

ingredients:

20g butter
1 small red capsicum (150g), sliced thinly
200g mushrooms, sliced thinly
2 tablespoons finely chopped fresh chives
8 eggs
1 tablespoon milk
4 green onions, sliced thinly
½ cup (60g) coarsely grated cheddar cheese

method:

1 Melt butter in large frying pan; cook capsicum, mushroom and chives, stirring occasionally, about 4 minutes or until vegetables soften. Drain vegetable filling on absorbent-paper-lined plate; cover with another plate or foil to keep warm.

2 Break eggs, one at a time, into small bowl then pour into a large jug. When all eggs are in jug, whisk until well combined and frothy, then whisk in milk and onion.

3 Pour half of the egg mixture into the frying pan you used for the vegetables; tilt pan to cover base with egg mixture. Cook over medium heat about 4 minutes or until omelette is just set.

4 Carefully spoon half of the vegetable filling onto one half of the omelette; sprinkle half of the cheese over vegetable filling. Use an egg slice to lift and fold the unfilled omelette half over the vegetable filling. Carefully slide omelette onto plate; cover with foil to keep warm.

5 Make one more omelette with remaining egg mixture, vegetable filling and cheese. Cut each omelette in half; place one half on each of four serving plates.

per serving 20.1g total fat (**9.3g** saturated fat); **1137kJ (272 cal); 3.1g** carbohydrate; **19.8g** protein; **1.9g** fibre

31

schoollunches

PREPARATION TIME 20 MINUTES (PLUS STANDING TIME) | COOKING TIME 25 MINUTES | MAKES 12

cheese, corn and bacon **muffins**

ingredients:

½ cup (85g) polenta
½ cup (125ml) milk
3 bacon rashers (210g), rind removed, chopped finely
4 green onions, chopped finely
1½ cups (225g) self-raising flour
1 tablespoon caster sugar
310g can corn kernels, drained
125g can creamed corn
100g butter, melted
2 eggs, beaten lightly
50g piece cheddar cheese
¼ cup (30g) coarsely grated cheddar cheese

method:

1 Preheat oven to moderately hot (200°C/180°C fan-forced). Oil 12-hole (⅓-cup/80ml) muffin pan.
2 Mix polenta and milk in small bowl; cover, stand 20 minutes.
3 Meanwhile, cook bacon, stirring, in heated small non-stick frying pan for 2 minutes. Add onion to pan; cook, stirring, for another 2 minutes. Remove pan from heat; cool bacon mixture about 5 minutes.
4 Sift flour and sugar into large bowl; stir in corn kernels, creamed corn and bacon mixture. Add melted butter, egg and polenta mixture; mix muffin batter only until just combined.
5 Spoon 1 tablespoon of the batter into each hole of the muffin pan. Cut the piece of cheese into 12 equal pieces, about the size of a 3cm cube; place one piece in the middle of the batter in muffin pan hole. Divide remaining batter among muffin pan holes; sprinkle grated cheese over each.
6 Bake, uncovered, about 20 minutes or until muffins are well-risen. Turn muffins onto wire rack. Serve muffins warm.

Only mix the muffin batter briefly, until just combined.

Place one cube of cheese into the centre of the muffin batter.

Turn muffins onto a wire rack to cool slightly, but serve them warm.

tip

➡ **Mix batter just enough to combine the ingredients, as overmixing can produce tough, heavy muffins. Corn is very nutritious, and is especially high in iron, necessary for healthy red blood cells.**

per muffin **13.3g** total fat (**7.4g** saturated fat); **1108kJ** (**265 cal**); **25.7g** carbohydrate; **9.8g** protein; **1.9g** fibre

tips

➡ **Baby spinach leaves can be used instead of the rocket if you like, and you can substitute sliced raw pumpkin for the kumara.**
➡ **To make a frittata that is lower in fat, replace the cream with a light (2 per cent fat) milk.**

per serving 25.6g total fat (**13.5g** saturated fat); **1593kJ (381 cal); 15.6g** carbohydrate; **21.6g** protein; **2g** fibre

PREPARATION TIME 15 MINUTES | COOKING TIME 1 HOUR | SERVES 6

○ vegetable **frittata**

A frittata is the Italian version of a filled omelette, the main difference being that it is oven-baked, while an omelette is cooked on top of the stove.

ingredients:

2 medium potatoes (400g), peeled, cut into 1cm slices
1 medium kumara (400g), peeled, cut into 1cm slices
10 eggs
½ cup (125ml) cream
1 cup (80g) coarsely grated parmesan cheese
½ cup (60g) coarsely grated cheddar cheese
50g baby rocket leaves
2 tablespoons thinly sliced fresh basil

method:

1 Preheat oven to moderate (180°C/160°C fan-forced). Grease deep 19cm-square cake pan; line base and sides with baking paper, bringing paper 5cm above edges.
2 Boil, steam or microwave potato and kumara, separately, until just tender; drain.
3 Meanwhile, break one egg into small bowl, then pour into large jug. Repeat with remaining eggs. When all eggs are in jug, whisk until well combined, then whisk in cream and both cheeses.
4 Layer potato slices in cake pan; top with rocket, then kumara slices, then basil. Carefully pour egg mixture over vegetables.
5 Bake frittata, covered, 45 minutes. Remove from oven; stand frittata in pan for 5 minutes before slicing into wedges.

Spread the rocket leaves over the potato.

Pour the egg mixture carefully over the vegetables so they stay in place.

Don't cut the frittata until it's been out of the oven for 5 minutes, to let it set.

tip

➡ Wholemeal and multigrain breads contain more fibre than white-flour breads, and also have more flavour.

PREPARATION TIME 10 MINUTES | MAKES 1

tuna and sweet corn sandwich

ingredients:

½ x 185g can tuna in springwater, drained
2 tablespoons drained and rinsed canned sweet corn kernels
1 tablespoon mayonnaise
2 slices bread
¼ Lebanese cucumber (30g), sliced thinly

method:

1 Combine tuna, corn and mayonnaise in small bowl.
2 Spread mixture on one slice of bread.
3 Top with cucumber and another slice of bread.

per sandwich **9.7g** total fat (**1.7g** saturated fat); **1379kJ** (**330 cal**); **34.4g** carbohydrate; **24.4g** protein; **3g** fibre

PREPARATION TIME 10 MINUTES | MAKES 3

chicken salad sandwiches

ingredients:

1½ cups (240g) finely chopped cooked chicken
4 green onions, sliced thinly
2 tablespoons pecans, chopped finely
½ trimmed celery stalk (50g), chopped finely
¼ cup (75g) mayonnaise
6 slices wholemeal bread
60g rocket

method:

1 Combine chicken, onion, nuts, celery and mayonnaise in medium bowl.
2 Spread a third of the chicken mixture on one slice of bread; top with rocket and another slice of bread. Repeat with remaining chicken mixture, bread and rocket to make two more sandwiches, or refrigerate remaining chicken mixture in an airtight container for up to two days.

per sandwich **19.2g** total fat (**3.2g** saturated fat); **1668kJ** (**399 cal**); **31.1** carbohydrate; **25.4g** protein; **2.9g** fibre

PREPARATION TIME 20 MINUTES | COOKING TIME 30 MINUTES | MAKES 12

pizza **scrolls**

ingredients:

2 cups (300g) self-raising flour
1 tablespoon caster sugar
30g butter
¾ cup (180ml) milk
¼ cup (70g) tomato paste
2 teaspoons Italian herb blend
100g sliced mild salami, cut into thin strips
1 medium green capsicum (200g), cut into thin strips
2 cups (200g) coarsely grated pizza cheese

method:

1 Preheat oven to moderate (180°C/160°C fan-forced). Grease 19cm x 29cm slice pan.

2 Place flour and sugar in medium bowl; use fingers to rub butter into flour mixture until it resembles coarse breadcrumbs. Stir in milk; mix to a soft, sticky dough. Knead dough lightly on floured surface. Using rolling pin, roll dough out to form 30cm x 40cm rectangle.

3 Using back of large spoon, spread tomato paste all over base, then sprinkle evenly with herb blend; top with salami, capsicum then cheese.

4 Starting from one of the long sides, roll dough up tightly; trim edges. Using serrated knife, cut roll carefully into 12 even slices; place slices, cut-side up, in single layer, in pan. Bake scroll slices, uncovered, about 30 minutes or until browned lightly.

Use fingertips to rub butter into flour.

Starting from one of the long sides, roll the dough tightly.

Use a serrated knife to slice roll; place slices in pan as they're cut.

per scroll **9.8g** total fat (**5.1g** saturated fat); **890kJ**
(**213 cal**); **20.9g** carbohydrate; **10g** protein; **1.3g** fibre

PREPARATION TIME 10 MINUTES | MAKES 1 LITRE (4 CUPS)

○ pineapple orange **frappé**

ingredients:
- 1 medium pineapple (1.25kg), chopped coarsely
- ½ cup (125ml) orange juice
- 3 cups crushed ice
- 1 tablespoon finely grated orange rind

method:

1 Blend or process pineapple and juice, in batches, until smooth.
2 Pour into large jug with crushed ice and rind; stir to combine.
Serve immediately.

per 250ml 0.2g total fat (**0g** saturated fat); **334kJ**
(**80 cal**); **15.7g** carbohydrate; **1.8g** protein; **3.6g** fibre

42

PREPARATION TIME 5 MINUTES | COOKING TIME 3 MINUTES | SERVES 4

banana, peanut butter and honey **crumpets**

ingredients:
- 8 crumpets
- ⅓ cup (95g) peanut butter
- 2 medium bananas (400g), sliced thinly
- ⅓ cup (115g) honey

method:
1 Preheat grill.
2 Toast crumpets. Spread with peanut butter, top with banana then drizzle with honey.
3 Place crumpets on oven tray under grill until honey starts to sizzle.

per serving **12.8g** total fat (**2.1g** saturated fat); **2036kJ** (**487 cal**); **78.3g** carbohydrate; **12.8g** protein; **6.3g** fibre

PREPARATION TIME 20 MINUTES | SERVES 4

○ morning trifles

tip

➡ Cereals and bran are high in fibre, a type of carbohydrate that provides energy.

ingredients:

⅓ cup (25g) All-Bran
⅓ cup (20g) Special K
⅓ cup (5g) puffed wheat
250g strawberries, hulled
1 cup (280g) vanilla yogurt
⅓ cup (80ml) passionfruit pulp

method:

1 Combine cereals in small bowl.
2 Cut six strawberries in half; reserve. Slice remaining strawberries thinly.
3 Divide half of the cereal mixture among four 1-cup (250ml) serving bowls; divide half of the yogurt, all the strawberry slices and half of the passionfruit pulp among bowls. Continue layering with remaining cereal and yogurt; top with reserved strawberry halves and remaining passionfruit pulp.

per serving 7.1g total fat (**1.6g** saturated fat); **577kJ** (**138 cal**); 16.6g carbohydrate; 7.1g protein; 6.3g fibre

44

tip

➡ Pancetta, an Italian unsmoked bacon, can be used, sliced or chopped, as an ingredient in recipes rather than eaten on its own. It's also great used as a pizza topping.

PREPARATION TIME 10 MINUTES | COOKING TIME 10 MINUTES | SERVES 4

○ pancetta and eggs

ingredients:

8 slices pancetta (120g)
2 green onions, sliced thinly
4 eggs
4 thick slices white bread, toasted

method:

1 Preheat oven to moderately hot (200°C/180°C fan-forced). Grease four holes of 12-hole (1/3-cup/80ml) muffin pan.

2 Line each of the muffin pan holes with 2 slices of the pancetta, overlapping to form a cup shape. Divide onion among pancetta cups. Break one egg into small bowl then slide it into a pancetta cup; repeat with remaining eggs.

3 Bake, uncovered, about 10 minutes or until eggs are just cooked and pancetta is crisp around the edges. Carefully remove from pan; serve with toast.

per serving **10.3g** total fat (**3.3g** saturated fat); **924kJ** (**221 cal**); **16.2g** carbohydrate; **15.4g** protein; **1.1g** fibre

drinks+juices

PREPARATION TIME 5 MINUTES | MAKES 1 LITRE (4 CUPS)

○ chocolate malted **milkshake**

ingredients: ⅓ cup (40g) malted milk powder
⅓ cup (80ml) chocolate-flavoured topping
1 cup (250ml) chocolate ice-cream
2½ cups (625ml) milk

method: **1** Blend or process all ingredients until smooth.

per 250ml 10.4g total fat (**6.6g** saturated fat); **1087kJ**
(**260 cal**); 35.5g carbohydrate; **7.8g** protein; **0g** fibre

PREPARATION TIME 5 MINUTES | MAKES 1 LITRE (4 CUPS)

○ **strawberry milkshake**

ingredients: · 250g strawberries, chopped coarsely
2 cups (500ml) milk
2 scoops strawberry ice-cream
½ cup (125ml) strawberry-flavoured topping

method: · **1** Blend or process all ingredients until smooth.

per 250ml **8.5g** total fat (**5.5g** saturated fat); **1007kJ**
(**241 cal**); **35.3g** carbohydrate; **6.5g** protein; **1.6g** fibre

tips

➤ Ask an adult to show you how to properly use a blender or food processor for your first few attempts.
➤ Many different fruits can be used in smoothies: use what's in season – that's when it's at its best and cheapest.

PREPARATION TIME 10 MINUTES | MAKES 1 LITRE (4 CUPS)

○ fruit tango **smoothie**

ingredients:

1 medium mango (430g), peeled, chopped coarsely
1 medium banana (200g), peeled, chopped coarsely
2 medium strawberries, hulls removed
200g honey and vanilla yogurt
1 cup (250ml) milk
10 ice-cubes
2 teaspoons honey
1 scoop vanilla ice-cream

method:

1 Blend or process all ingredients until smooth.

per 250ml 6g total fat (**3.8g** saturated fat); **857kJ (205 cal)**; **30.4g** carbohydrate; **6.6g** protein; **2g** fibre

tip

➡ **Use overripe bananas for more sweetness; never use underripe fruit because it doesn't puree.**

PREPARATION TIME 5 MINUTES | MAKES 3 CUPS

○ banana **smoothie**

ingredients:
- 2 medium bananas (400g), peeled, chopped coarsely
- 1 cup (250ml) milk
- 1 tablespoon honey
- 8 ice-cubes
- 1 scoop vanilla ice-cream

method:
1 Blend or process all ingredients until smooth.

per 250ml **5.6g** total fat (**3.6g** saturated fat); **853kJ** (**204 cal**); **33.8g** carbohydrate; **5.1g** protein; **2g** fibre

PREPARATION TIME 10 MINUTES | SERVES 1

◯ **pineapple, orange and strawberry juice**

ingredients:

1 small orange (180g), peeled, quartered
150g pineapple, chopped coarsely
2 strawberries
¼ cup (60ml) water

method:

1 Push orange, pineapple and strawberries through juice extractor into glass; stir in the water.

per serving **0.2g** total fat (**0g** saturated fat); **389kJ** (**93 cal**); **7.4g** carbohydrate; **2.7g** protein; **4.9g** fibre

PREPARATION TIME 5 MINUTES | SERVES 1

○ **watermelon juice**

ingredients: 450g watermelon, seeds removed, chopped coarsely
4 fresh mint leaves

method: **1** Blend or process all ingredients until smooth;
pour into glass.

per serving **1g** total fat (**0g** saturated fat); **464kJ**
(**111 cal**); **2.7g** carbohydrate; **1.5g** protein; **3.1g** fibre

afterschoolsnacks

after-school snacks

PREPARATION TIME 5 MINUTES | COOKING TIME 5 MINUTES | SERVES 2

○ mexican **bagels**

ingredients:
1 bagel
1 tablespoon bottled salsa
½ small avocado (100g), sliced thickly
2 slices cheddar cheese

method:
1 Preheat grill.
2 Split bagel in half horizontally; spread 2 teaspoons of salsa over each half. Top each half with avocado and one cheese slice.
3 Place under grill about 5 minutes or until cheese melts.

per bagel half **15.6g** total fat (**6.1g** saturated fat); **1354kJ** (**324 cal**); **32.3g** carbohydrate; **12.3g** protein; **2.6g** fibre

did you know?

The avocado is a tropical fruit that contains fat but no cholesterol. Apart from the olive, it is the only high-fat fruit, but because it's monounsaturated (the heart-healthy "good" fat we also get from olive oil) it may actually help lower cholesterol. Rich in antioxidants (substances that protect the body against cell damage), avocados are also a good source of vitamins B6 and E, dietary fibre, potassium and essential fatty acids.

tip

➡ Try spreading ripe
and creamy avocado
on your sandwiches
instead of butter.

➡ Unripe avocados
will soften and be
ready to eat sooner
if they are kept at
room temperature
rather than in
the refrigerator.

tip

➡ **Both of these recipes are best if they are made a day ahead and left overnight in the freezer.**

PREPARATION TIME 5 MINUTES (PLUS FREEZING TIME) | MAKES 6

○ frozen fruit and yogurt **blocks**

ingredients:

1½ cups (420g) vanilla yogurt
1 cup (150g) frozen mixed berries
1 tablespoon honey

method:

1 Combine yogurt, berries and honey in medium bowl; spoon into six ¼-cup (60ml) ice-block moulds. Press lids on firmly; freeze 6 hours or overnight.

per block **2.4g** total fat (**1.5g** saturated fat); **380kJ** (**91 cal**); **12.5g** carbohydrate; **3.8g** protein; **1g** fibre

PREPARATION TIME 5 MINUTES (PLUS FREEZING TIME) | MAKES 6

○ vanilla-caramel swirl ice-cream **blocks**

ingredients:

1½ cups softened vanilla ice-cream
¼ cup (60ml) caramel-flavoured topping

method:

1 Spoon ice-cream into six ¼-cup (60ml) ice-block moulds.
2 Swirl 2 teaspoons topping into each mould. Press lids on
firmly; freeze 6 hours or overnight.

per block **2.7g** total fat (**1.9g** saturated fat); **322kJ**
(**77 cal**); **12.5g** carbohydrate; **1.2g** protein; **0.1g** fibre

PREPARATION TIME 10 MINUTES | COOKING TIME 10 MINUTES | MAKES 4

Spread pitta breads with tomato paste.

Sprinkle toppings on pizza.

tip

➡ **It's best if you don't assemble the pizzas until you are ready to cook them.**

○ mini **pizzas**

ingredients:

4 pitta pocket breads
⅓ cup (90g) tomato paste
150g cabanossi, sliced thinly
100g ham, chopped finely
½ medium red capsicum (100g), chopped finely
440g can pineapple pieces in natural juice, drained
1½ cups (180g) grated cheddar cheese

method:

1 Preheat oven to hot (220°C/200°C fan-forced).
2 Spread each pocket bread with 1 tablespoon of the tomato paste.
3 Place pocket breads onto oven trays; top with cabanossi, ham, capsicum and pineapple. Sprinkle with cheese.
4 Cook, uncovered, about 12 minutes or until cheese melts and is browned lightly.

per pizza 27.4g total fat (**14g** saturated fat); **2554kJ**
(**611 cal**); **56.9g** carbohydrate; **31.3g** protein; **5g** fibre

PREPARATION TIME 20 MINUTES | COOKING TIME 10 MINUTES | MAKES 24

Press down on pastry stack halves. **Cut pastry into 24 thin strips.** **Pinch ends of twists to seal.**

cheesy pastry **twists**

ingredients:

2 sheets ready-rolled puff pastry, thawed
1 egg yolk, beaten lightly
1 cup (100g) coarsely grated pizza cheese
½ cup (40g) finely grated parmesan cheese

method:

1 Preheat oven to moderately hot (200°C/180°C fan-forced). Oil two oven trays; line with baking paper.
2 Brush one pastry sheet with half of the egg yolk; sprinkle with pizza cheese. Top with remaining pastry sheet; brush with remaining egg yolk. Sprinkle with parmesan cheese.
3 Cut pastry stack in half; place one pastry half on top of the other, pressing down firmly.
4 Cut pastry widthways into 24 strips; twist each, pinching ends to seal. Place twists on trays.
5 Bake, uncovered, about 10 minutes or until browned lightly.

per twist **4.8g** total fat (**1.2g** saturated fat); **314kJ** (**75 cal**); **5g** carbohydrate; **2.7g** protein; **0.2g** fibre

dinnerforthefamily

PREPARATION TIME 20 MINUTES | COOKING TIME 45 MINUTES | SERVES 4

Add peas carefully to soup to make sure it doesn't splash.

minestrone

ingredients:

1 tablespoon olive oil

4 bacon rashers (280g), chopped coarsely

2 medium brown onions (300g), sliced thickly

2 cloves garlic, crushed

1 medium carrot (120g), chopped coarsely

2 small potatoes (240g), chopped coarsely

2 trimmed celery stalks (200g), chopped coarsely

1.5 litres (6 cups) beef stock

400g can chopped tomatoes

2 tablespoons tomato paste

1 cup macaroni (150g)

½ cup frozen peas (60g)

1 cup finely shredded cabbage (80g)

2 small zucchini (180g), chopped coarsely

method:

1 Heat oil in large saucepan; cook bacon, onion, garlic, carrot, potato and celery, stirring, about 5 minutes or until onion is soft.

2 Add stock, undrained tomatoes and tomato paste. Bring to a boil; reduce heat, simmer, covered, about 30 minutes or until vegetables are tender, stirring occasionally.

3 Add macaroni, peas, cabbage and zucchini; boil, uncovered, about 10 minutes or until pasta is just tender. Serve minestrone with warm bread rolls, if desired.

per serving **11.6g** total fat (**3g** saturated fat); **1689kJ** (**404 cal**); **48g** carbohydrate; **22g** protein; **8.7g** fibre

tip

➡ Remember that the more different coloured foods you use in a dish, the healthier it is. Bright colours in natural foods like tomatoes, cabbage, carrots, peas and zucchini show they contain antioxidants, thought to prevent disease.

PREPARATION TIME 10 MINUTES | COOKING TIME 5 MINUTES | SERVES 4

Cut chicken into 1cm strips.

◯ chicken noodle **soup**

ingredients:

3 cups (750ml) chicken stock
1 litre (4 cups) water
3 chicken breast fillets (600g), cut into 1cm strips
310g can corn kernels, drained
2 teaspoons soy sauce
2 x 85g packets chicken-flavoured 2-minute noodles
1 tablespoon chopped fresh chives

method:

1 Combine stock and the water in large saucepan, bring to
a boil; add chicken, corn, sauce, the chicken-flavour sachet
from the noodles and the noodles to the pan.
2 Bring soup back to a boil, turn the heat to medium and
cook about 5 minutes or until chicken is cooked through.
3 Serve soup sprinkled with chives.

per serving 10.3g total fat (**3.1g** saturated fat); **1852kJ**
(**443 cal**); **43.5g** carbohydrate; **41.8g** protein; **3.2g** fibre

dinner for the family

◯ mixed salad

ingredients:

8 cos lettuce leaves
1 medium avocado (250g)
1 Lebanese cucumber (130g), sliced thinly
250g cherry tomatoes, cut in half
1 medium carrot (120g), peeled, cut into matchsticks

dressing
½ cup (125ml) olive oil
¼ cup (60ml) lemon juice
1 teaspoon dijon mustard
2 teaspoons caster sugar

method:

1 Tear lettuce leaves into bite-sized pieces.
2 Cut avocado in half lengthways (cutting around the seed), then twist the halves to separate them from the seed. Scoop out the seed with a spoon, then carefully peel skin away from the avocado. Cut avocado into slices.
3 Combine lettuce, avocado, cucumber, tomato and carrot in large salad bowl.
4 Pour dressing over salad; toss gently to combine.

dressing
Place all ingredients in a glass jar. Screw the lid on tightly and shake well.

After scooping out the seed, slice the avocado with a sharp knife.

Make sure the lid is on tight when you shake the jar with the salad dressing.

tip

➡ Five servings of vegetables a day are recommended to sustain good health. Serving sizes are largely based on age and appetite, but a general rule is that they are individually determined by what can be held in the palm of one hand.

per serving 28.8g total fat
(**4g** saturated fat); **1229kJ** (**294 cal**);
4.6g carbohydrate; **2.6g** protein; **4.1g** fibre

tip

➡ A healthy change from the deep-fried version, oven-baked fish 'n' chips is lower in fat but certainly no less delicious.

per serving 66.1g total fat (**9.7g** saturated fat); **4753kJ** (**1137 cal**); 88.7g carbohydrate; **43.7g** protein; **6.6g** fibre

PREPARATION TIME 35 MINUTES | COOKING TIME 35 MINUTES | SERVES 4

oven-baked fish 'n' chips with tartare **sauce**

ingredients:

1kg potatoes, peeled
cooking-oil spray
8 firm white fish fillets (750g)
¼ cup (35g) plain flour
3 egg whites, beaten lightly
1 tablespoon milk
2¼ cups (155g) stale breadcrumbs
¾ cup (120g) cornflake crumbs

tartare sauce

2 egg yolks
1 tablespoon lemon juice
½ teaspoon mustard powder
1 cup (250ml) vegetable oil
2 tablespoons milk, approximately
2 tablespoons chopped gherkins
2 tablespoons drained rinsed
    capers, chopped
2 tablespoons chopped fresh chives

method:

1 Preheat oven to moderately hot (200°C/180°C fan-forced).
2 Cut potatoes into 1.5cm slices; cut slices into 1cm chips. Place chips, in single layer, on lightly greased oven tray; spray lightly with cooking-oil spray. Bake, uncovered, about 35 minutes or until brown.
3 Meanwhile, working with one fish fillet at a time, toss fish in flour, shake off excess; dip fish into combined egg white and milk, then combined crumbs. Place on oiled oven tray; repeat with remaining fish.
4 Bake fish, uncovered, for the final 20 minutes of chip baking time.
5 Serve fish 'n' chips with tartare sauce.

tartare sauce Blend or process egg yolks, juice and mustard until smooth. With motor operating, gradually add oil, in thin steady stream; process until sauce thickens. Place in serving bowl; whisk in only enough milk to give desired consistency, stir in remaining ingredients.

Cut potatoes into slices; try to get each slice the same width.

Coat the chips lightly with cooking-oil spray before baking them.

One fillet at a time, dip fish into flour, egg white and milk, then combined crumbs.

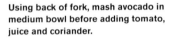

Using back of fork, mash avocado in medium bowl before adding tomato, juice and coriander.

PREPARATION TIME 15 MINUTES ┊ COOKING TIME 15 MINUTES ┊ SERVES 4

steak sandwich with guacamole

ingredients:

2 tablespoons olive oil

2 medium brown onions (300g), sliced thinly

4 beef minute steaks (400g)

1 large avocado (320g)

2 medium tomatoes (300g), seeded, chopped finely

1 tablespoon lime juice

1 tablespoon finely chopped fresh coriander

4 small Turkish breads, split horizontally

8 butter lettuce leaves

method:

1 Heat half of the oil in large frying pan; cook onion, stirring, about 5 minutes or until browned lightly. Remove from pan; cover with foil to keep warm.

2 Heat remaining oil in same pan; cook beef, two at a time, until browned both sides and cooked as desired. Remove from pan; cover with foil to keep warm.

3 To make guacamole, use fork to mash avocado in medium bowl; add tomato, juice and coriander, mix gently to combine.

4 Toast cut sides of bread. Place bottom halves of bread on serving plates; top with equal amounts of lettuce, then beef, onion, guacamole and remaining toasted bread tops.

per serving 33.1g total fat (**7.3g** saturated fat); **3248kJ** (**777 cal**); **76.7g** carbohydrate; **38.6g** protein; **7.7g** fibre

tip

➡ **You can use lavash or pitta bread instead of the mountain bread, if you prefer.**
➡ **Middle-Eastern spice mix is available from Middle Eastern food stores and most supermarkets.**

PREPARATION TIME 15 MINUTES | COOKING TIME 10 MINUTES | SERVES 4

spiced beef and hummus wraps

ingredients:

800g thick beef boneless sirloin steaks
2 tablespoons Middle-Eastern spice mix
4 pieces mountain bread
½ cup (130g) hummus
1 baby cos lettuce (180g)
2 large egg tomatoes (180g), sliced thickly
¼ cup (70g) Greek-style yogurt

method:

1 Trim excess fat from beef. Sprinkle beef with Middle-Eastern spice mix.
2 Cook beef on heated, oiled grill pan (or barbecue or pan-fry) about 5 minutes on each side or until cooked as desired. Stand 5 minutes then slice beef thinly.
3 To serve, spread bread with hummus, top with lettuce, tomato, beef and yogurt; wrap to enclose.

per serving **19.4g** total fat (**6.7g** saturated fat); **2366kJ** (**566 cal**); **41.2g** carbohydrate; **53.2g** protein; **6.2g** fibre

PREPARATION TIME 20 MINUTES | COOKING TIME 40 MINUTES | SERVES 4

oven-baked chicken schnitzel with spicy **wedges**

ingredients:

1kg potatoes, washed
1 egg white, beaten lightly
¼ teaspoon cayenne pepper
½ teaspoon sweet paprika
4 chicken thigh fillets (440g)
⅓ cup (50g) plain flour
2 egg whites, beaten lightly, extra
½ cup (50g) packaged breadcrumbs
½ cup (80g) cornflake crumbs

method:

1 Preheat oven to hot (220°C/200°C fan-forced).
2 Cut unpeeled potatoes into wedges. Combine potato, egg white, cayenne pepper and paprika in large bowl; toss to coat potato all over in spice mixture. Place potato, in single layer, in shallow, lightly oiled baking dish. Bake, uncovered, about 40 minutes or until browned lightly.
3 Meanwhile, trim fat from chicken. Using meat mallet, gently pound chicken until 5mm thick. Toss chicken in flour; shake away excess.
4 Dip chicken in small bowl containing extra egg white then toss in separate small bowl containing combined crumbs. Place chicken, in single layer, on oiled oven tray. Bake, uncovered, about 20 minutes or until browned both sides and cooked through.
5 Serve chicken schnitzel with spicy potato wedges.

Use a sharp knife to cut potatoes into wedges.

Pound chicken with meat mallet until 5mm thin.

Dip chicken into combined crumbs to cover chicken completely.

tip

➡ Serve the chicken schnitzel with lime wedges, a bowl of sweet chilli sauce and a green salad dressed with lemon vinaigrette.

per serving **5.6g** total fat (**1.5g** saturated fat); **1898kJ** (**454 cal**); **62.1g** carbohydrate; **35g** protein; **5g** fibre

tip

➡ **Ask an adult to help you drain the spaghetti. If you make the bolognese sauce a day before you want to eat it, the flavour will be better.**

per serving 9.4g total fat (**2.7g** saturated fat); **2023kJ** (**484 cal**); **65.9g** carbohydrate; **29.9g** protein; **6.2g** fibre

PREPARATION TIME 15 MINUTES | COOKING TIME 50 MINUTES | SERVES 6

Cook beef, stirring, until browned.   **Stir carrot and zucchini into bolognese.**   **Drain spaghetti before serving.**

spaghetti **bolognese**

ingredients:

1 tablespoon olive oil
1 large brown onion (200g), chopped finely
1 clove garlic, crushed
500g beef mince
2 x 400g cans chopped tomatoes
⅓ cup (90g) tomato paste
1 cup (250ml) beef stock
1 medium carrot (120g), grated coarsely
1 small zucchini (90g), grated coarsely
500g spaghetti

method:

1 Heat oil in large saucepan, add onion and garlic; cook, stirring, about 5 minutes or until onion is soft.

2 Add beef, stir with a wooden spoon about 5 minutes or until browned all over.

3 Add undrained tomatoes, tomato paste, stock, carrot and zucchini to pan. Stir bolognese sauce with a wooden spoon to mix together. Bring to a boil; reduce heat, simmer, uncovered, about 30 minutes or until sauce thickens slightly, stirring occasionally.

4 Meanwhile, cook spaghetti, uncovered, in large saucepan of boiling water about 10 minutes or until just tender; drain.

5 Serve bolognese sauce spooned over hot spaghetti. Serve sprinkled with parmesan cheese, if desired.

79

PREPARATION TIME 20 MINUTES | COOKING TIME 35 MINUTES | SERVES 4

Cook rissoles both sides until browned and cooked through.

Roughly crush potatoes by smashing them briefly with a potato masher.

Cook the flour in same pan until mixture bubbles and thickens.

lamb rissoles with potato crush and rosemary gravy

ingredients:

500g lamb mince
1 large brown onion (200g), grated coarsely
1 clove garlic, crushed
1 egg, beaten lightly
½ cup (35g) stale breadcrumbs
1 tablespoon olive oil
500g new potatoes
20g butter
1 tablespoon plain flour
1 cup (250ml) beef stock
1 tablespoon chopped fresh rosemary leaves
250g cherry tomatoes

method:

1 Using hands, combine lamb, onion, garlic, egg and breadcrumbs in medium bowl. Shape lamb mixture into eight patties.

2 Heat oil in large frying pan; cook rissoles both sides, about 15 minutes or until browned and cooked through. Drain on absorbent paper; cover with foil to keep warm. Reserve pan with rissole drippings.

3 Meanwhile, boil, steam or microwave potatoes until tender; drain. Crush potatoes in medium bowl by smashing them a few times with potato masher; stir in butter.

4 To make rosemary gravy, add flour to rissole pan; cook, stirring, until mixture browns and bubbles. Gradually stir in stock; stir until gravy boils and thickens. Strain gravy; stir in rosemary.

5 Meanwhile, cook tomatoes, stirring, in heated small frying pan about 2 minutes or until split and just softened.

6 Divide potato among serving plates, top with rissoles, rosemary gravy and tomatoes.

per serving **21.7g** total fat (**8.9g** saturated fat); **1856kJ**
(**444 cal**); **26.4g** carbohydrate; **33.7g** protein; **3.9g** fibre

◯ marinated pork ribs

ingredients:

4 slabs (1.2kg) American-style pork ribs
⅓ cup (80ml) plum sauce
2 tablespoons barbecue sauce
2 tablespoons tomato sauce
1 tablespoon soy sauce

method:

1 Place pork in large shallow glass dish, pour over combined sauces; turn pork to coat in marinade. Cover, refrigerate 3 hours or overnight.
2 Preheat oven to moderately hot (200°C/180°C fan-forced).
3 Remove pork from marinade; reserve marinade. Place pork, in a single layer, on wire rack over baking dish (you might need two dishes).
4 Cook pork, uncovered, 20 minutes. Brush pork with reserved marinade; cook further 20 minutes or until cooked through.

Pour combined sauces over slabs of pork in large shallow glass dish; turn pork slabs to coat in marinade.

tip

➡ **A slab of American-style pork spareribs will consist of between 7 and 10 ribs each. After the meat is cooked, separate the ribs with a knife then eat them in your hands.**

per serving 11.1g total fat (**3.6g** saturated fat); **1271kJ** (**304 cal**); **22.2g** carbohydrate; **29.1g** protein; **0.5g** fibre

dinner for the family

Shape beef mixture into four patties that are roughly the same size.

Cook beef patties until they are browned and cooked through.

cheeseburgers

ingredients:

500g beef mince

1 medium brown onion (150g), grated coarsely

1 teaspoon dried mixed herbs

2 tablespoons barbecue sauce

½ cup (50g) packaged breadcrumbs

1 egg, beaten lightly

¼ cup (60ml) olive oil

4 hamburger buns, cut in half

4 lettuce leaves

2 medium egg tomatoes (150g), sliced thinly

½ x 450g can sliced beetroot, drained

4 slices cheddar cheese

¼ cup (60ml) tomato sauce

method:

1 Combine beef, onion, herbs, barbecue sauce, breadcrumbs and egg in large bowl. Shape mixture into four patties.

2 Heat oil in large frying pan, add patties; cook over medium heat about 15 minutes or until browned both sides and cooked through. Remove patties from pan; drain on absorbent paper.

3 Preheat grill.

4 Toast buns, cut-side up, under grill. Layer bottom half of bun with lettuce, tomato, beetroot, patties, cheese and tomato sauce. Top with remaining bun.

tip

➡ Use the best-quality, low-fat beef mince
you can find to make these burgers.

per burger **32.4g** total fat
(**10.2g** saturated fat); 2997kJ (**717 cal**);
60.6g carbohydrate; **43.3g** protein; **6.2g** fibre

tip

➡ **You need eight 20cm wooden skewers for the satay sticks; soak them in cold water for at least an hour before using to prevent them from splintering when you thread on the meat and to stop them from scorching when being cooked.**

per serving 45.7g total fat (**12.2g** saturated fat); **4105kJ** (**982 cal**); **88.5g** carbohydrate; **50.3g** protein; **8.2g** fibre

PREPARATION TIME 25 MINUTES | COOKING TIME 20 MINUTES | SERVES 4

○ pork **satay**

ingredients:

¾ cup (210g) smooth peanut butter
⅓ cup (80ml) coconut cream
¼ cup (60ml) sweet chilli sauce
⅓ cup (80ml) chicken stock
1 tablespoon lime juice
500g pork strips
2 cups (400g) white long-grain rice
3 cups (750ml) boiling water
¼ cup (35g) coarsely chopped, roasted unsalted peanuts
⅓ cup coarsely chopped fresh coriander

method:

1 Preheat oven to moderate (180°C/160°C fan-forced).
2 Combine peanut butter, coconut cream, chilli sauce, stock and juice in small bowl.
3 Thread pork strips onto eight skewers. Place skewers, in single layer, in large shallow baking dish; spoon peanut sauce over pork. Bake, uncovered, about 20 minutes or until pork is cooked through.
4 Meanwhile, place rice in medium saucepan with the boiling water, stir until water returns to a boil; cover with tightly fitting lid. Cook rice over low heat for 15 minutes without removing lid. Remove from heat; stand rice in pan, still covered, for 5 minutes.
5 Divide rice among serving dishes; top with satay sticks then peanut sauce from baking dish, sprinkle with peanuts and coriander.

Thread the pork strips onto eight skewers then place in baking dish.

Spoon the peanut sauce evenly over the pork skewers in dish.

dinner for the family

PREPARATION TIME 25 MINUTES | COOKING TIME 25 MINUTES | SERVES 4

Spread cooked rice on a tray in an
even layer and refrigerate until cold.

Swirl egg carefully along side
of wok to make omelette.

Give a final gentle toss
to fried rice to combine.

○ fried rice

ingredients:

3 teaspoons peanut oil

2 eggs, beaten lightly

1 teaspoon sesame oil

4 bacon rashers (280g),
  chopped coarsely

1 medium brown onion (150g),
  chopped coarsely

2 trimmed celery stalks (200g),
  sliced thickly

1 clove garlic, crushed

4cm piece fresh ginger (20g),
  grated finely

3 cups cold cooked white long-grain rice

100g shelled, cooked small prawns

425g can baby corn, drained, sliced

½ cup frozen peas (60g), thawed

4 green onions, sliced thinly

1 tablespoon soy sauce

method:

1 Heat one teaspoon of the peanut
oil in hot wok; add half of the egg,
swirl wok to make a thin omelette.
Remove omelette from wok; roll
omelette, cut into thin strips. Repeat
using another teaspoon of the
peanut oil and remaining egg.

2 Heat remaining peanut oil and
the sesame oil in wok; stir-fry bacon
about 3 minutes or until brown.
Add onion, celery, garlic and
ginger; stir-fry over high heat
about 3 minutes or until vegetables
are just tender.

3 Add rice, omelette and remaining
ingredients to wok; stir-fry until well
combined and heated through.

tip

➡ One cup of long-grain rice will make 3 cups of cooked rice. Cook it the day before you need it. This will prevent the grains from sticking together as you make the fried rice.

➡ Boil 1 cup (200g) of rice, uncovered, in a large saucepan of water until the rice is just tender. Drain rice then spread it on a tray, cover with absorbent paper; refrigerate overnight.

per serving **17.2g** total fat (**5.1g** saturated fat); **1898kJ** (**454 cal**); **46.2g** carbohydrate; **25.8g** protein; **5.4g** fibre

tip

➡ This recipe is high in carbohydrates, substances your body uses to provide you with lots of energy. Besides pasta, other carbohydrate-rich foods include rice, potatoes and breads.

➡ We've used angel-hair pasta (also sold as "capelli d'angelo") instead of traditional wide lasagne sheets.

per serving **24.9g** total fat (**12.9g** saturated fat); **1655kJ** (**396 cal**); **27.5g** carbohydrate; **13.2g** protein; **5.6g** fibre

PREPARATION TIME 25 MINUTES | COOKING TIME 50 MINUTES | SERVES 6

Spread the wilted silver beet over sheets of absorbent paper to drain.

Mash the pumpkin mixture until it is almost like mashed potato.

Cover pasta sauce with remaining pasta.

vegetable lasagne

ingredients:

400g piece pumpkin, peeled, chopped coarsely
500g silver beet, trimmed, chopped coarsely
150g angel hair pasta
2 tablespoons olive oil
1 small leek (200g), sliced thinly
²⁄₃ cup (160ml) vegetable stock
¾ cup (120g) ricotta cheese
¾ cup (180ml) cream
1½ cups (390g) bottled tomato pasta sauce
¾ cup (75g) coarsely grated pizza cheese

method:

1 Preheat oven to moderate (180°C/160°C fan-forced).
2 Boil, steam or microwave pumpkin until just tender; boil, steam or microwave silver beet until slightly wilted. Drain vegetables separately. Mash pumpkin in small bowl; reserve. Spread silver beet over sheets of absorbent paper, cover with more absorbent paper; reserve.
3 Meanwhile, cook pasta in medium saucepan of boiling water about 5 minutes or until just tender; drain. Rinse under cold water; drain.
4 Heat oil in medium saucepan; cook leek, stirring, about 5 minutes or until softened. Add pumpkin and stock; cook, uncovered, stirring occasionally, about 5 minutes or until liquid is absorbed.
5 Meanwhile, combine silver beet in medium bowl with ricotta and cream.
6 Spread pumpkin mixture over the bottom of 2-litre (8-cup) shallow baking dish; cover pumpkin mixture with half of the pasta. Spread sauce over pasta; cover with remaining pasta.
7 Pour silver beet mixture over pasta, gently spreading to completely cover pasta. Sprinkle pizza cheese all over surface of lasagne.
8 Place lasagne on oven tray. Bake, uncovered, about 30 minutes or until lasagne is heated through and cheese is browned lightly.

dinner**for**mum

PREPARATION TIME 5 MINUTES | MAKES 2½ CUPS

○ **beetroot dip**

tip

ingredients:
825g can beetroot slices, drained
1 clove garlic
¼ cup (60g) sour cream
1 tablespoon lemon juice

method:
1 Blend or process all ingredients until smooth. Serve with toasted Turkish bread, if desired.

per tablespoon **0.8g** total fat (**0.5g** saturated fat); **71kJ** (**17 cal**); **1.8g** carbohydrate; **0.3g** protein; **0.5g** fibre

➡ **Serve with a selection of fresh vegetable sticks or water crackers.**
➡ **Beetroot dip can be made a day ahead; keep, covered, in refrigerator.**

PREPARATION TIME 25 MINUTES | COOKING TIME 10 MINUTES | SERVES 4

○ veal campagnola

ingredients:

300g spinach
4 veal steaks (500g)
¼ cup (35g) plain flour
30g butter
1 tablespoon olive oil
500ml bottled tomato pasta sauce
250g mozzarella cheese, cut into
    4 slices

method:

1 Remove and discard stems from spinach; rinse leaves under cold water to remove grit. Drain; rinse again. Place spinach in colander to allow excess water to drain away.
2 Place each piece of veal between pieces of plastic wrap; pound evenly and firmly until veal steaks are of the same thickness. Discard plastic wrap.

3 Toss veal steaks in flour, one at a time, coating both sides evenly; shake away excess flour.
4 Place a large frying pan (with a tight-fitting lid) over high heat; add butter. When butter starts to sizzle, add all the spinach; cover immediately, turn off heat. Stand spinach 3 minutes without lifting lid.
5 Return wilted spinach to colander to drain; wipe out pan with absorbent paper. Place pan over high heat, add oil; cook veal, uncovered, until browned both sides. Drain on absorbent paper.
6 Add pasta sauce to same pan; bring to a boil then reduce heat. Carefully place veal steaks, in single layer, on sauce; top each steak with a quarter of the spinach and a cheese slice. Cover; simmer about 1 minute or until cheese melts.
7 Serve veal campagnola with a mixed green salad.

per serving 27.8g total fat (**14.4g** saturated fat); **2119kJ (507 cal)**; 14.9g carbohydrate; **47.2g** protein; **4.1g** fibre

PREPARATION TIME 15 MINUTES | COOKING TIME 1 HOUR | SERVES 4

roast pumpkin and potato with garlic and rosemary

ingredients:

750g butternut pumpkin, chopped coarsely
750g medium potatoes, chopped coarsely
1 tablespoon olive oil
2 cloves garlic, sliced thinly
2 tablespoons fresh rosemary leaves
2 teaspoons sea salt

method:

1 Preheat oven to hot (220°C/200°C fan-forced).
2 Combine pumpkin, potato, oil and garlic in large baking dish.

3 Roast, uncovered, about 1 hour or until vegetables are just tender and browned lightly.
4 Serve sprinkled with rosemary and salt.

per serving 5.7g total fat (**1.1g** saturated fat); **899kJ (215 cal)**; **31.1g** carbohydrate; **7g** protein; **4.7g** fibre

94

PREPARATION TIME 10 MINUTES ┆ COOKING TIME 25 MINUTES ┆ SERVES 4

○ sour cherry baked custards

ingredients:

1 cup (200g) drained morello cherries
3 eggs
1 teaspoon vanilla extract
½ cup (110g) caster sugar
2 cups (500ml) hot milk
2 teaspoons custard powder
1 tablespoon cold milk
½ teaspoon ground cinnamon

method:

1 Preheat oven to moderately slow (170°C/150°C fan-forced).
2 Pat cherries dry with absorbent paper; divide among four shallow 1-cup (250ml) ovenproof dishes. Place dishes on baking tray.

3 Whisk eggs, extract and sugar in large jug. Gradually whisk hot milk into egg mixture.
4 Blend custard powder with cold milk in small bowl until smooth; whisk into egg mixture. Pour mixture over cherries.
5 Bake, uncovered, about 25 minutes or until just set. Serve warm or cooled sprinkled with cinnamon.

per serving **9.1g** total fat (**4.6g** saturated fat); **1241kJ** (**297 cal**); **43.0g** carbohydrate; **9.9g** protein; **0.9g** fibre

desserts

PREPARATION TIME 25 MINUTES (PLUS REFRIGERATION TIME) | SERVES 6

Line the dish with sponge pieces to make the bottom of the trifle flat.

Carefully pour the jelly mixture onto the sponge pieces in the dish.

Using a spatula, spread the cream mixture over trifle.

○ berry trifle with mousse **filling**

ingredients:

200g packaged sponge cake, chopped coarsely
85g packet strawberry jelly crystals
1 cup (250ml) boiling water
½ cup (125ml) cold water
500g packet frozen mixed berries
100g packet vanilla instant pudding mix
2¾ cups (680ml) cold milk
½ cup (125ml) thickened cream
2 teaspoons icing sugar

method:

1 Line bottom of deep round 2-litre (8-cup) serving dish with the sponge to make the bottom of the trifle a flat surface.

2 Combine jelly crystals with the boiling water in large jug, stirring, until jelly dissolves; stir in the cold water. Measure ¾ cup of the frozen berries, cover; place in the refrigerator. Stir remaining berries into jelly mixture.

3 Carefully pour jelly mixture over top of sponge pieces without moving the sponge pieces. Cover; refrigerate about 2 hours or until jelly sets.

4 Sprinkle pudding mix over milk in large bowl; whisk until combined. Pour pudding mixture over set jelly; refrigerate, covered, about 30 minutes or until pudding mixture sets.

5 Beat cream and icing sugar in small bowl with electric mixer until soft peaks form. Using rubber spatula, spread cream over trifle; sprinkle with reserved drained berries.

per serving **4.8g** total fat (**8.9g** saturated fat); **1643kJ**
(**393 cal**); **55.5g** carbohydrate; **10.1g** protein; **2.5g** fibre

tips

➡ **Start making this recipe at least 5 hours before you want to eat it to ensure the mousse has plenty of time to firm.**

➡ **Care must be taken when heating the chocolate mixture: if the heat is too high, the chocolate will "seize", that is, become clumpy, grainy and unusable.**

per serving **56.1g** total fat (**36.4g** saturated fat); **3219kJ** (**770 cal**); **59.5g** carbohydrate; **11.4g** protein; **0.1g** fibre

PREPARATION TIME 10 MINUTES | COOKING TIME 5 MINUTES (PLUS COOLING TIME) | SERVES 4

⬡ white chocolate and honeycomb **mousse**

ingredients:

2 eggs, separated
250g white eating chocolate, chopped coarsely
1 tablespoon caster sugar
1 teaspoon gelatine
⅓ cup (80ml) milk
300ml thickened cream
2 x 50g chocolate-coated honeycomb bars, chopped coarsely

method:

1 Place egg yolks, chocolate, sugar, gelatine and milk in small heavy-based saucepan; stir continuously, over low heat, until mixture is smooth. Transfer mixture to large bowl; cool.
2 Beat egg whites, in small bowl, with electric mixer until soft peaks form.
3 Beat cream, in separate small bowl, with electric mixer until soft peaks form.
4 Fold cream and honeycomb into chocolate mixture, then fold in egg whites. Divide mixture among four 1-cup (250ml) serving glasses; refrigerate mousse, covered, for 4 hours before serving.

Make sure there is no trace of yolk when beating egg whites, otherwise the mixture won't form soft peaks.

Fold the combined whipped cream and honeycomb into the white chocolate mixture.

PREPARATION TIME 20 MINUTES ┃ COOKING TIME 10 MINUTES (PLUS COOLING TIME) ┃ SERVES 4

○ spiced apple fillo cups

ingredients:

425g can pie apple
½ teaspoon ground cinnamon
¼ teaspoon ground nutmeg
½ cup (35g) stale breadcrumbs
¾ cup (120g) sultanas
1 ½ tablespoons caster sugar
4 sheets fillo pastry
30g butter, melted
1 tablespoon icing sugar

method:

1 Preheat oven to moderately hot (200°C/180°C fan-forced). Grease eight holes of a 12-hole (⅓-cup/80ml) muffin pan.
2 Combine apple, cinnamon, nutmeg, breadcrumbs, sultanas and caster sugar in medium bowl.

3 Place one pastry sheet on board; brush with a little of the butter, then top with another pastry sheet. Repeat brushing and layering with remaining butter and pastry sheets.
4 Cut fillo stack down the centre vertically; cut into quarters horizontally (you will have eight rectangles). Press one fillo stack into each of the eight greased holes of the muffin pan (four holes remain empty during baking).
5 Divide apple evenly among pastry cases.
6 Bake, uncovered, about 10 minutes or until pastry is browned lightly.
7 Using spatula, carefully remove fillo cups from pan; cool 5 minutes on wire rack, dust with sifted icing sugar.

Brush one pastry sheet with a little of the butter.

After cutting the fillo stacks, you will have eight rectangles.

Press the fillo rectangles into eight holes of the muffin pan.

per serving 7.1g total fat (**4.2g** saturated fat); **1333kJ**
(**319 cal**); **59.5g** carbohydrate; **4.1g** protein; **3.7g** fibre

per serving 41.1g total fat (**26.7g** saturated fat); **2826kJ**
(**676 cal**); **70.3g** carbohydrate; **11.4g** protein; **2.5g** fibre

PREPARATION TIME 5 MINUTES | COOKING TIME 5 MINUTES | SERVES 6

Stir chocolate sauce constantly over very low heat until just melted.

Top sundaes with equal parts pink and white marshmallows just before serving.

tip

▶ **Make quick banana splits by cutting half a banana into wheels over the top of each sundae.**

○ chocolate **sundaes**

ingredients:

2 litres vanilla ice-cream
½ cup (70g) crushed nuts
12 ice-cream wafers
100g marshmallows

hot chocolate sauce
200g dark eating chocolate, chopped coarsely
½ cup (125ml) thickened cream

method:

1 Make hot chocolate sauce.
2 Place a little of the hot chocolate sauce in the bottom of six ¾-cup (180ml) serving glasses; top with ice-cream, more chocolate sauce, nuts, wafer biscuits and marshmallows.

hot chocolate sauce
Combine chocolate and cream in small saucepan; stir over low heat until chocolate is melted and sauce is smooth, do not overheat.

PREPARATION TIME 15 MINUTES | COOKING TIME 25 MINUTES | SERVES 6

➡ **You can substitute pear for the apple, if you like, or even a single berry variety.**
➡ **Fresh or frozen berries can be used.**

Use fingertips to rub butter into muesli mixture.

Sprinkle muesli mixture evenly over apple mixture.

○ apple and berry **crumble**

ingredients:

800g can pie apple
2 cups (300g) frozen mixed berries
1 tablespoon white sugar
½ cup (125ml) water
1 cup (130g) toasted muesli
2 tablespoons plain flour
1 tablespoon brown sugar
50g butter, chopped
½ cup (20g) cornflakes

method:

1 Preheat oven to moderate (180°C/160°C fan-forced).
2 Combine apple, berries, white sugar and the water in medium saucepan. Bring to a boil; reduce heat, simmer, stirring, until mixture is combined. Remove from heat.
3 Meanwhile, combine muesli, flour and brown sugar in medium bowl. Use fingertips to rub in butter; stir in cornflakes.
4 Place apple mixture in 2-litre (8-cup) ovenproof dish; sprinkle with muesli mixture.
5 Bake, uncovered, about 20 minutes or until browned lightly. Serve with custard or ice-cream, if desired.

per serving 9.2g total fat (**5.2g** saturated fat); **1112kJ**
(**266 cal**); **40.5g** carbohydrate; **3.7g** protein; **5.3g** fibre

per serving **16.9g** total fat (**11.3g** saturated fat); **1898kJ**
(**454 cal**); **71.1g** carbohydrate; **5.8g** protein; **2g** fibre

PREPARATION TIME 10 MINUTES | COOKING TIME 15 MINUTES | SERVES 8

Pour syrup mixture evenly over pudding mixture.

microwave cherry-ripe self-saucing **pudding**

ingredients:

60g butter, chopped
1½ cups (225g) self-raising flour
1 cup (220g) caster sugar
⅓ cup (35g) cocoa powder
1¼ cups (310ml) milk
1 teaspoon vanilla extract
2 x 55g Cherry Ripe bars, chopped coarsely
½ cup (110g) firmly packed brown sugar
1 tablespoon cocoa powder, extra
2 cups (500ml) boiling water
50g butter, chopped, extra

method:

1 Melt butter in deep 3-litre (12-cup) microwave-safe dish, uncovered, on HIGH (100%) in microwave oven about 1 minute. Using oven mitts, remove dish from microwave oven.
2 Add sifted flour, caster sugar and cocoa to dish with milk and extract; whisk until smooth. Stir in Cherry Ripe.
3 Combine brown sugar and sifted extra cocoa in medium jug; gradually stir in the boiling water. Add extra butter; stir until butter melts. Carefully pour syrup mixture evenly over pudding mixture.
4 Cook, uncovered, on HIGH (100%) in microwave oven about 15 minutes or until just cooked in centre. Using oven mitts, remove dish from microwave oven; stand 5 minutes before serving with cream, if you like.

desserts

PREPARATION TIME 5 MINUTES (PLUS COOLING AND REFRIGERATION TIME) | SERVES 6

○ jelly custard **cups**

ingredients:

2 cups (500ml) boiling water
85g packet strawberry jelly crystals
600ml carton prepared custard
3 strawberries, halved

method:

1 Pour the boiling water into a large heatproof jug. Sprinkle jelly crystals into jug, stir until crystals are dissolved and mixture is clear; cool.
2 Place six ¾-cup (180ml) serving glasses on a tray. Pour jelly evenly into glasses.
3 Pour custard slowly over the jelly. Leave the glasses on the tray, cover each with plastic wrap; put the tray in the refrigerator for about 4 hours or until the jelly is set.
4 Just before serving, place a strawberry half on top of each jelly cup.

per serving **3.4g** total fat (**2.2g** saturated fat); **669kJ** (**160 cal**); **28.6g** carbohydrate; **4.8g** protein; **0.2g** fibre

PREPARATION TIME 20 MINUTES (PLUS STANDING TIME) | COOKING TIME 10 MINUTES (PLUS COOLING TIME) | SERVES 6

○ orange butterscotch **fondue**

ingredients:

⅔ cup (150g) firmly packed brown sugar
25g butter
⅔ cup (160ml) cream
1 teaspoon finely grated orange rind
2 tablespoons orange juice
100g white eating chocolate, chopped coarsely
1 large banana (230g), chopped coarsely
250g strawberries, halved
2 small pears (360g), chopped coarsely
2 medium mandarins (400g), segmented
18 marshmallows

method:

1 Stir sugar, butter, cream, rind and juice in medium saucepan until sugar dissolves. Bring to a boil; boil, uncovered, 3 minutes. Remove from heat; cool 5 minutes.
2 Stir in chocolate until fondue mixture is smooth; stand 5 minutes. Transfer to serving bowl.
3 Arrange fruit and marshmallows on serving platter; serve with fondue and skewers for dipping.

per serving **20.7g** total fat (**13.4g** saturated fat); **1822kJ** (**436 cal**); **61.6g** carbohydrate; **4g** protein; **3.3g** fibre

PREPARATION TIME 10 MINUTES | COOKING TIME 10 MINUTES | SERVES 4

layered banana split with caramel **sauce**

ingredients:

⅔ cup (160ml) thickened cream
60g butter
¾ cup (165g) firmly packed brown sugar
1 cup (250ml) thickened cream, extra
500ml vanilla ice-cream
2 large bananas (460g), sliced thinly
½ cup (40g) almond flakes, toasted

method:

1 Stir cream, butter and sugar in small saucepan, over medium heat, until smooth. Reduce heat; simmer, uncovered, 2 minutes. Cool 10 minutes.
2 Meanwhile, beat extra cream in small bowl with electric mixer until soft peaks form.
3 Divide half of the sauce among four serving dishes; top with ice-cream, cream, banana, remaining sauce and nuts.

per serving 62.2g total fat (**37.9g** saturated fat); **3616kJ** (**865 cal**); **71.4g** carbohydrate; **7.8g** protein; **2.6g** fibre

tips

➡ **Bananas are a good source of the minerals potassium, which helps our brains function properly, and phosphorous, essential for good health. They are also a great source of easy-to-digest fibre.**
➡ **Don't peel or cut the bananas until you're just ready to assemble this dessert because they'll turn brown quickly.**

Stir cream, butter and sugar in small saucepan.

PREPARATION TIME 15 MINUTES (PLUS REFRIGERATION TIME) | COOKING TIME 20 MINUTES | SERVES 4

Push the blackberry mixture through sieve into small bowl.

Gently fold the blackberry mixture into the egg whites.

blackberry **soufflés**

> ➡ **Folding egg whites or whipped cream into other mixtures must be done carefully, using a large spoon or spatula. Take care to turn the spoon over gently so that you don't deflate the aerated whites or cream.**

ingredients:

300g frozen blackberries
1 tablespoon water
⅓ cup (75g) caster sugar
4 egg whites
1 tablespoon icing sugar

method:

1 Preheat oven to moderately hot (200°C/180°C fan-forced).
2 Combine blackberries and the water in small saucepan; bring to a boil. Reduce heat; simmer, uncovered, until blackberries soften. Add caster sugar, stir over medium heat, without boiling, until sugar dissolves; bring to a boil. Reduce heat; simmer, uncovered, 5 minutes. Remove from heat; using the back of a large spoon, push blackberry mixture through sieve into small bowl, discarding seeds in the sieve. Refrigerate 15 minutes.
3 Beat egg whites in a medium bowl with electric mixer until soft peaks form. Fold in the blackberry mixture until combined.
4 Divide mixture among four lightly greased 1-cup (250ml) ovenproof dishes; place on oven tray. Bake, uncovered, about 12 minutes or until soufflés are puffed and browned lightly. Dust with sifted icing sugar; serve immediately.

per serving **0.2g** total fat (**0g** saturated fat); **439kJ**
(**105 cal**); **20.6g** carbohydrate; **3.4g** protein; **3.5g** fibre

per serving **14.1g** total fat (**9.2g** saturated fat); **1037kJ**
(**248 cal**); **27.6g** carbohydrate; **3g** protein; **1.5g** fibre

PREPARATION TIME 20 MINUTES (PLUS REFRIGERATION TIME) | SERVES 8

tip

➡ **If mangoes are in season, you can use one weighing about 600g for this recipe. Peel it over a small bowl to catch as much juice as possible, then cut off mango cheeks and slice the cheeks thinly. Squeeze as much juice as possible from around the seed into bowl with other juice; add enough cold water to make 1 cup cold liquid to add to the jelly (step 2).**

Pour the raspberry jelly carefully over raspberries and chilled mango jelly.

○ mango and raspberry jelly

ingredients:

425g can sliced mango
85g packet mango jelly crystals
2 cups (500ml) boiling water
150g raspberries
85g packet raspberry jelly crystals
1 cup (250ml) cold water
300ml thickened cream

method:

1 Drain mango in sieve over small bowl; reserve liquid. Measure ¼ cup mango slices and reserve. Divide remaining mango slices among eight ¾-cup (180ml) glasses.
2 Combine mango jelly crystals with 1 cup of the boiling water in small bowl, stirring until jelly dissolves. Add enough cold water to reserved mango liquid to make 1 cup of liquid; stir into mango jelly. Divide evenly among glasses over mango, cover; refrigerate about 2 hours or until jelly sets.
3 Divide raspberries among glasses over set jelly. Combine raspberry jelly crystals and remaining cup of the boiling water in small bowl, stirring until jelly dissolves; stir in the cold water. Divide evenly among glasses over raspberries, cover; refrigerate about 2 hours or until jelly sets.
4 Beat cream in small bowl with electric mixer until soft peaks form. Spread cream equally among glasses; top with reserved mango.

tip

➡ **Turkish bread is also called pide by some bakers and in some supermarkets. It is also available in individual rounds.**

PREPARATION TIME 15 MINUTES | SERVES 4

○ bruschetta **caprese**

ingredients:

1 long loaf Turkish bread
30g baby rocket leaves
250g cherry tomatoes, halved
100g baby bocconcini cheese, sliced thickly
2 tablespoons finely shredded fresh basil
1 tablespoon extra virgin olive oil

method:

1 Halve bread; reserve one half for another use. Cut remaining half crossways into four even-width pieces. Split each piece horizontally; toast both sides.

2 Place two bread slices on each serving plate. Top each slice with equal amounts of rocket, tomato, cheese and basil; drizzle with oil.

per serving **12g** total fat (**3.7g** saturated fat); **1568kJ** (**375 cal**); **49.6g** carbohydrate; **14.4g** protein; **4g** fibre

118

PREPARATION TIME 10 MINUTES | COOKING TIME 25 MINUTES | SERVES 4

○ garlic and sage lamb **racks**

ingredients:

- 3 large red onions (900g)
- 12 fresh sage leaves
- ⅓ cup (80ml) olive oil
- 2 tablespoons coarsely chopped fresh sage
- 4 cloves garlic, chopped coarsely
- 4 x 4 French-trimmed lamb cutlet racks (600g)

method:

1 Preheat oven to hot (220°C/200°C fan-forced).

2 Halve onions, slice into thin wedges; place in large baking dish with whole sage leaves and half of the oil.

3 Combine remaining oil in small bowl with chopped sage and garlic. Press sage mixture all over lamb; place on onion in dish.

4 Roast, uncovered, about 25 minutes or until lamb is browned all over and cooked as desired. Cover lamb racks; stand 10 minutes before serving.

per serving 31.3g total fat (**8.5g** saturated fat); **1701kJ** (**407 cal**); **12.4g** carbohydrate; **18.4g** protein; **3.4g** fibre

PREPARATION TIME 5 MINUTES | **COOKING TIME** 10 MINUTES | **SERVES** 4

tip

○ parmesan mash

ingredients:

- 4 medium potatoes (800g), peeled, chopped coarsely
- 30g butter
- ½ cup (125ml) milk
- ⅔ cup (50g) finely grated parmesan cheese

method:

1 Boil, steam or microwave potato until soft; drain.

2 Mash potato in large bowl with remaining ingredients until smooth.

➡ Potato mash can be made several hours ahead, covered and refrigerated. Reheat on LOW (10%) in a microwave oven just before serving.

per serving 11.6g total fat (**7.4g** saturated fat); **1032kJ** (**247 cal**); **24g** carbohydrate; **10g** protein; **2.7g** fibre

tip

➡ **To fold the cream and egg whites into the chocolate mousse mixture, use a large flat rubber spatula.**

PREPARATION TIME 15 MINUTES | COOKING TIME 3 MINUTES (PLUS REFRIGERATION TIME) | SERVES 4

○ chocolate and nougat mousse

ingredients:
- 200g Toblerone chocolate, chopped coarsely
- 2 eggs, separated
- ½ cup (125ml) thickened cream

method:

1 Place 150g of the chocolate in microwave-safe bowl; cook on MEDIUM-LOW (30%) in microwave oven for 1 minute. Using oven mitts, remove bowl from microwave oven; stir chocolate, return bowl to microwave oven. Repeat cooking and stirring until chocolate is melted. Cool slightly, stir in the egg yolks.

2 Meanwhile, beat cream in small bowl with electric mixer until soft peaks form. Fold whipped cream into chocolate mixture.

3 Beat egg whites in clean small bowl with electric mixer until soft peaks form. Fold into the chocolate mixture.

4 Spoon into ¾-cup (180ml) serving glasses. Refrigerate mousse for 3 hours or overnight.

5 Garnish with the remaining chopped chocolate before serving.

per serving **28.5g** total fat (**16.9g** saturated fat); **1689kJ** (**404 cal**); **32.4g** carbohydrate; **6.5g** protein; **0.6g** fibre

baking

PREPARATION TIME 15 MINUTES | COOKING TIME 15 MINUTES | MAKES 16

○ buttermilk **scones**

ingredients:

3 cups (450g) self-raising flour
1 teaspoon icing sugar
60g butter, chopped
1¾ cups (430ml) buttermilk
300ml thickened cream
¾ cup (240g) strawberry jam

method:

1 Preheat oven to hot (220°C/200°C fan-forced). Grease and flour 23cm-square slab cake pan.

2 Combine flour, icing sugar and butter in food processor; process until mixture resembles breadcrumbs. Add buttermilk; process until just combined (mixture should be sticky). Turn dough onto floured surface, knead lightly until smooth. Press dough out into 3cm thickness. Using a 5.5cm round cutter, cut dough into 16 rounds. (You will need to gently re-roll the dough to get the 16 rounds.)

3 Place scones into pan; they will fit comfortably, just touching one another slightly. Bake, uncovered, about 20 minutes or until browned lightly.

4 Beat cream in small bowl with electric mixer until thickened.

5 Serve warm scones, cut in half, topped with jam and cream.

Blend or process mixture with buttermilk.

Knead dough lightly on floured surface until smooth.

Cut dough into 16 rounds. Place rounds, barely touching, in pan.

per half scone with jam and cream
10.9g total fat (**7g** saturated fat); **978kJ**
(**234 cal**); **29.1g** carbohydrate;
4.4g protein; **1.2g** fibre

tips

➡ It is important not to overmix muffin mixture; it should be slightly lumpy.
➡ If you are using frozen berries, use them unthawed; this will minimise "bleeding" of the colour into the mixture.

per muffin **9.6g** total fat (**6.4g** saturated fat); **1170kJ** (**280 cal**); **42.8g** carbohydrate; **5.1g** protein; **2.3g** fibre

PREPARATION TIME 10 MINUTES | COOKING TIME 20 MINUTES | MAKES 12

Rub butter into flour with fingertips.   **Mix muffin mixture until just combined.**   **Sprinkle coconut on muffin mix.**

○ raspberry and coconut **muffins**

ingredients:

2½ cups (375g) self-raising flour
90g butter, chopped
1 cup (220g) caster sugar
1¼ cups (310ml) buttermilk
1 egg, beaten lightly
⅓ cup (25g) desiccated coconut
150g fresh or frozen raspberries
2 tablespoons shredded coconut

method:

1 Preheat oven to moderately hot (200°C/180°C fan-forced). Grease 12-hole (⅓-cup/80ml) muffin pan.

2 Place flour in large bowl; using fingertips, rub in butter. Add sugar, buttermilk, egg, desiccated coconut and raspberries; using fork, mix until just combined.

3 Divide mixture among pan holes; sprinkle with shredded coconut.

4 Bake, uncovered, about 20 minutes. Stand muffins 5 minutes before turning, top-side up, onto wire rack to cool.

baking

PREPARATION TIME 10 MINUTES | COOKING TIME 15 MINUTES | MAKES 12

○ mini strawberry **friands**

ingredients:

2 egg whites
60g butter, melted
⅓ cup (40g) almond meal
½ cup (80g) icing sugar
2 tablespoons plain flour
2 small strawberries, sliced thinly

method:

1 Preheat oven to moderately hot (200°C/180°C fan-forced). Grease 12-hole (1 tablespoon/20ml) mini muffin pan.
2 Place egg whites in small bowl, whisk lightly; add butter, almond meal, sifted icing sugar and flour. Whisk until just combined. Divide mixture among pan holes. Top each with a strawberry slice.
3 Bake, uncovered, about 15 minutes. Turn, top-side up, onto wire rack to cool. Serve warm or at room temperature, dusted with extra sifted icing sugar, if desired.

Whisk egg whites lightly with a wire whisk.

Spoon mixture into prepared pan holes.

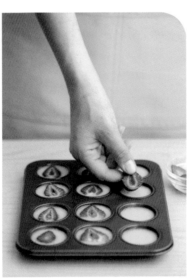
Place a strawberry slice on top of each friand before baking.

tips

➡ Strawberries are
jam-packed with the good
health-promoting vitamins
A and C. Bet you didn't
know that they are the only
fruit that has its seeds on
the outside.

per friand **6g** total fat (**2.8g** saturated fat); **380kJ**
(**91 cal**); **8.2g** carbohydrate; **1.4g** protein; **0.4g** fibre

PREPARATION TIME 20 MINUTES | COOKING TIME 10 MINUTES PER TRAY | MAKES 36

Beat the butter, extract, sugar and egg in small bowl until smooth.

Place level tablespoons of the mixture, 5cm apart, on trays.

chunky chocolate-chip **cookies**

ingredients:

125g butter, softened
1 teaspoon vanilla extract
1¼ cups (275g) firmly packed brown sugar
1 egg
1 cup (150g) plain flour
¼ cup (35g) self-raising flour
½ teaspoon bicarbonate of soda
⅓ cup (35g) cocoa powder
½ cup (100g) peanut M&M's
⅓ cup (70g) mini M&M's
½ cup (75g) milk chocolate melts

method:

1 Preheat oven to moderate (180°C/160°C fan-forced). Lightly grease two oven trays.
2 Beat butter, extract, sugar and egg in small bowl with electric mixer until smooth (do not overmix). Transfer mixture to large bowl; mix in sifted combined dry ingredients then all chocolates.
3 Place level tablespoons of the mixture onto trays, allowing 5cm between each cookie. Bake, uncovered, about 10 minutes. Stand cookies 5 minutes; transfer to wire rack to cool.

per cookie **4.9g** total fat (**2.9g** saturated fat); **451kJ** (**108 cal**); **15.1g** carbohydrate; **1.5g** protein; **0.3g** fibre

PREPARATION TIME 30 MINUTES | COOKING TIME 20 MINUTES | MAKES 24

butterfly cakes

ingredients:

125g butter, softened
1 teaspoon vanilla extract
⅔ cup (150g) caster sugar
3 eggs
1½ cups (225g) self-raising flour
¼ cup (60ml) milk
½ cup (160g) strawberry jam
300ml thickened cream, whipped
4 strawberries, sliced thinly
1 tablespoon icing sugar

method:

1 Preheat oven to moderate (180°C/160°C fan-forced). Line two deep 12-hole patty pans with paper cases.
2 Combine butter, extract, caster sugar, eggs, flour and milk in small bowl of electric mixer; beat on low speed until ingredients are just combined. Increase speed to medium, beat about 3 minutes or until mixture is smooth and changed to a paler colour.
3 Drop slightly rounded tablespoons of mixture into paper cases. Bake, uncovered, about 20 minutes. Turn cakes, top-side up, onto wire racks to cool.
4 Using sharp pointed vegetable knife, cut circle from top of each cake; cut circle in half to make two "wings". Fill cavities with jam and whipped cream. Place wings in position on top of cakes; top with strawberry slices and dust with a little sifted icing sugar.

Spoon the mixture into paper cases.

Cut small circles from tops of cakes.

Fill the cavities with jam and cream.

tips

➡ Use two paper patty cases in each patty pan hole for added stability for butterfly cakes.
➡ Cakes are at their best made on the day of serving. Once filled with the cream, refrigerate the cakes if you're not going to eat them right away.

per cake 9.8g total fat (**6.2g** saturated fat); **702kJ** (**168 cal**); **18.3g** carbohydrate; **2.2g** protein; **0.5g** fibre

tips

➡ To make a slightly different variation of this slice, try adding ¾ cup dark chocolate Bits, ¾ cup sultanas, or ¾ cup finely chopped dried apricots in with the oats (step 2).
➡ This recipe is a great lunchbox treat. It will keep in an airtight container for up to four days, so you can make it on the weekend to take to school.

per piece **4.6g** total fat (**3.1g** saturated fat); **422kJ** (**101 cal**); **14g** carbohydrate; **1g** protein; **0.6g** fibre

PREPARATION TIME 20 MINUTES | COOKING TIME 35 MINUTES (PLUS STANDING TIME) | MAKES 30

○ anzac **slice**

ingredients:

1 cup (90g) rolled oats
1 cup (150g) plain flour
1 cup (220g) firmly packed brown sugar
½ cup (40g) desiccated coconut
125g butter, chopped coarsely
2 tablespoons golden syrup
1 tablespoon water
½ teaspoon bicarbonate of soda

method:

1 Preheat oven to moderately slow (170°C/150°C fan forced). Grease 26cm x 32cm Swiss roll pan; line base and two long sides with baking paper.

2 Combine oats, flour, sugar and coconut in large bowl.

3 Combine butter, golden syrup and the water in medium saucepan; stir mixture with a wooden spoon until butter is melted.

4 Remove pan from heat. Add soda to the butter mixture (it will froth and bubble).

5 Pour butter mixture into oat mixture and stir with a wooden spoon until all the ingredients are mixed together. Spoon mixture evenly into pan, then press down on the slice with your hands until it is flat.

6 Bake, uncovered, about 30 minutes (it should feel firm when you touch it).

7 Stand slice in pan about 15 minutes. Turn slice out of pan, remove baking paper, then cut slice into pieces while still warm.

Add bicarbonate of soda to butter mixture; it will froth.

Pour butter mixture over oat mixture then stir with a wooden spoon.

Using your hands, press mixture flat into Swiss roll pan.

PREPARATION TIME 25 MINUTES | COOKING TIME 30 MINUTES | MAKES 20

○ apricot muesli **slice**

ingredients:

100g butter, softened
½ cup (110g) caster sugar
1 egg yolk
⅔ cup (100g) plain flour
¼ cup (35g) self-raising flour
1 tablespoon custard powder
½ cup (160g) apricot jam, warmed

muesli topping
¼ cup (90g) honey
50g butter
1½ cups (135g) rolled oats
1 cup (40g) cornflakes
½ cup (40g) shredded coconut
½ cup (80g) finely chopped dried apricots

method:

1 Preheat oven to moderate (180°C/160°C fan-forced). Grease 20cm x 30cm lamington pan; line base and two long sides with baking paper, extending paper 2cm above sides.

2 Beat butter, sugar and egg yolk in small bowl with electric mixer until light and fluffy. Stir in sifted combined flours and custard powder. Using fingers, press mixture over base of pan.
3 Bake, uncovered, about 15 minutes or until browned lightly.
4 Meanwhile, make muesli topping.
5 Remove slice from oven, spread with jam. Press muesli topping over jam, pressing gently with fingers. Return to oven; bake a further 15 minutes.
6 Cool slice in pan before cutting into 20 pieces to serve.

muesli topping
Heat honey and butter in small saucepan until butter melts; transfer to large bowl. Stir in remaining ingredients.

Grease lamington pan, then line with baking paper.

Use fingers to press slice mixture over the base of prepared pan.

Using fingers, gently press the muesli topping onto the base.

per piece **8.4g** total fat (**5.4g** saturated fat); **811kJ**
(**194 cal**); **27.6g** carbohydrate; **2.1g** protein; **1.5g** fibre

tips

➡ Choose a level-bottomed baking dish, not one with ridges; one made from cast aluminium is the best choice, but almost any type will work.
➡ If the cake appears to be cooking too quickly in the corners, reduce oven temperature to moderately slow (170°C/150°C fan-forced); this will increase the cooking time by up to 15 minutes.

per serving **15.8g** total fat (**9.8g** saturated fat); **1756kJ** (**420 cal**); **67.3g** carbohydrate; **4.3g** protein; **1g** fibre

PREPARATION TIME 20 MINUTES | COOKING TIME 1 HOUR (PLUS COOLING AND REFRIGERATION TIME) | SERVES 20

family chocolate cake with fudge **frosting**

ingredients:

2 cups (500ml) water
3 cups (660g) caster sugar
250g butter, chopped
⅓ cup (35g) cocoa powder
1 teaspoon bicarbonate of soda
3 cups (450g) self-raising flour
4 eggs, beaten lightly

fudge icing
90g butter
⅓ cup (80ml) water
½ cup (110g) caster sugar
1½ cups (240g) icing sugar
⅓ cup (35g) cocoa powder

method:

1 Preheat oven to moderate (180°C/160°C fan-forced). Grease deep 26.5cm x 33cm (14-cup/3.5-litre) baking dish; line base with baking paper.
2 Combine the water, sugar, butter and combined sifted cocoa and soda in medium saucepan; stir over heat, without boiling, until sugar dissolves. Bring to a boil; reduce heat; simmer, uncovered, 5 minutes. Transfer mixture to large bowl; cool to room temperature.
3 Add flour and egg to mixture; beat with electric mixer until mixture is smooth and changed to a paler colour. Pour mixture into dish.
4 Bake, uncovered, about 50 minutes. Stand cake 10 minutes before turning, top-side up, onto wire rack to cool.
5 Spread cold cake with fudge icing.

fudge icing
Combine butter, the water and caster sugar in small saucepan; stir over heat, without boiling, until sugar dissolves. Sift icing sugar and cocoa into small bowl then gradually stir in hot butter mixture. Cover; refrigerate about 20 minutes or until icing thickens. Beat with wooden spoon until spreadable.

Simmer water, sugar, butter, cocoa and soda until sugar dissolves.

Pour cake mixture evenly into prepared baking dish.

PREPARATION TIME 35 MINUTES ┃ COOKING TIME 55 MINUTES (PLUS COOLING TIME) ┃ SERVES 10

banana **cake**

ingredients:

125g butter, softened
¾ cup (150g) firmly packed
   brown sugar
2 eggs
1½ cups (225g) self-raising flour
½ teaspoon bicarbonate of soda
1 teaspoon mixed spice
1 cup mashed banana
½ cup (120g) sour cream
¼ cup (60ml) milk

cream cheese icing
1 cup (160g) icing sugar
250g cream cheese

method:

1 Preheat oven to moderate (180°C/160°C fan-forced). Grease 15cm x 25cm loaf pan; line base with baking paper.

2 Beat butter and sugar in small bowl with electric mixer until light and fluffy. Beat in eggs, one at a time, until combined. Transfer mixture to large bowl; using wooden spoon, stir in sifted dry ingredients, banana, sour cream and milk. Spread mixture into pan.

3 Bake cake about 50 minutes. Stand cake 5 minutes before turning, top-side up, onto wire rack to cool.

4 Spread cold cake with cream cheese icing.

cream cheese icing
Beat sifted icing sugar and cream cheese in small bowl, on medium speed, with electric mixer until mixture is smooth.

Use a fork to mash ripe bananas.

Using a plastic spatula, spread mixture into prepared pan.

Spread cold cake evenly with cream cheese frosting.

tips

You need two large overripe bananas for this recipe because they mash easily and are the most flavourful. If the bananas you buy are not ripe enough, put them in a paper bag and keep them at room temperature for a day or two.

per serving 24.9g total fat (**15.7g** saturated fat); **1898kJ** (**454 cal**); **52.4g** carbohydrate; **6.7g** protein; **1.4g** fibre

tips

➡ **There are many types of food colourings available including pastes, gels, powders and liquids. Since they all vary greatly in strength, start tinting by using only a drop or a tiny amount, then increase the amount until you get the depth of colour you desire.**

per serving 30.8g total fat (**19.5g** saturated fat); **2119kJ** (**507 cal**); **52.6g** carbohydrate; **6.4g** protein; **1.3g** fibre

PREPARATION TIME 30 MINUTES | COOKING TIME 1 HOUR (PLUS COOLING TIME) | SERVES 10

○ marble **cake**

ingredients:

250g butter, softened
1 teaspoon vanilla extract
1¼ cups (275g) caster sugar
3 eggs
2¼ cups (335g) self-raising flour
¾ cup (180ml) milk
pink food colouring
2 tablespoons cocoa powder
1 tablespoon milk, extra

pink butter icing
90g soft butter
1 cup (160g) icing sugar
1 tablespoon milk
pink food colouring

method:

1 Preheat oven to moderate (180°C/160°C fan-forced). Grease deep 22cm-round cake pan; line base with baking paper.
2 Beat butter, extract and sugar in medium bowl with electric mixer until light and fluffy. Add eggs, one at a time, beating until combined. Using wooden spoon, stir in flour and milk, in two batches.
3 Divide mixture evenly among three bowls; tint mixture in one bowl pink by stirring through a few drops of colouring with a wooden spoon.
4 Using a teaspoon, blend sifted cocoa with extra milk in a cup; stir into the second bowl of mixture.
5 Drop alternate spoonfuls of the three coloured mixtures into pan. Pull a skewer backwards and forwards through cake mixture several times for a marbled effect; smooth surface with metal spatula.
6 Bake, uncovered, about 1 hour. Stand cake 5 minutes before turning, top-side up, onto wire rack to cool.
7 Spread cold cake with pink butter icing.

pink butter icing
Beat butter in small bowl with electric mixer until light and fluffy; beat in icing sugar and milk. Tint with pink colouring.

Stir cocoa into one third of the cake mixture.

Drop spoonfuls of coloured mixture, alternately, into pan.

To marble the cake, pull a skewer back and forth through the mixture.

boys' tex-mex night

tip

➡ Place the minced beef mixture, taco shells, lettuce, cheese, tomato and salsa in separate bowls on the table, and let everyone assemble their own tacos.

➡ Eat nachos as soon as they're ready or the corn chips will go soggy.

PREPARATION TIME 15 MINUTES | COOKING TIME 25 MINUTES | MAKES 12

○ beef tacos

ingredients:

2 teaspoons olive oil
500g beef mince
1 clove garlic, crushed
1½ cups (375ml) water
2 tablespoons tomato paste
35g packet taco seasoning
12 taco shells
8 lettuce leaves, shredded finely
2 medium tomatoes (300g), chopped finely
1 cup (120g) grated cheddar cheese
½ cup bottled mild chunky salsa

per taco **10.9g** total fat (**3.9g** saturated fat); **874kJ** (**209 cal**); **12.7g** carbohydrate; **13.6g** protein; **2.9g** fibre

method:

1 Preheat oven to moderate (180°C/160°C fan-forced).

2 Heat oil in large frying pan, add beef and garlic; cook, stirring, about 5 minutes or until the beef is browned all over. Add the water, tomato paste and taco seasoning to beef mixture; stir until well combined. Bring to a boil; reduce heat, simmer, uncovered, about 10 minutes or until most of the liquid is evaporated.

3 Meanwhile, place taco shells, upside down, on oven tray. Heat shells in oven, uncovered, about 5 minutes or until heated through. Using oven mitts, remove tray from oven, place on a wooden board.

4 Divide beef mixture among taco shells; top with lettuce, tomato and cheese, drizzle with salsa.

PREPARATION TIME 15 MINUTES | COOKING TIME 35 MINUTES | SERVES 4

○ vegie nachos

ingredients:

1 tablespoon olive oil

1 medium brown onion (150g), chopped finely

1 clove garlic, crushed

400g can chopped tomatoes

420g can mexibeans, drained, rinsed

230g packet corn chips

1 cup (120g) grated cheddar cheese

½ cup (120g) sour cream

1 tablespoon chopped fresh coriander

method:

1 Preheat oven to moderately hot (200°C/180°C fan-forced).

2 Heat oil in medium frying pan; cook onion and garlic, stirring, about 5 minutes or until onion softens. Stir in undrained tomatoes and beans.

3 Bring mixture to a boil; reduce heat, simmer, uncovered, 15 minutes, stirring constantly, until mixture thickens slightly.

4 Place corn chips onto large ovenproof plate; pour bean mixture over chips, then sprinkle with cheese. Bake, uncovered, about 10 minutes or until cheese is melted. Serve topped with sour cream and coriander.

per serving **43.4g** total fat (**21.3g** saturated fat); **2867kJ** (**686 cal**); **49.3g** carbohydrate; **20.5g** protein; **13.3g** fibre

145

PREPARATION TIME 20 MINUTES | COOKING TIME 40 MINUTES | SERVES 4

○ potato wedges with **guacamole**

ingredients:

4 medium potatoes (800g), unpeeled
1 tablespoon olive oil
1 tablespoon chicken seasoning
cooking-oil spray

guacamole

3 medium avocados (750g)
½ small red onion (50g), chopped finely
1 small egg tomato (60g), seeded,
   chopped finely
1 tablespoon lime juice
¼ cup chopped fresh coriander

method:

1 Preheat oven to hot (220°C/200°C
fan-forced).
2 Wash and scrub the potatoes well; dry
with absorbent paper.

3 Cut potatoes in half; cut each half into
wedges. Combine wedges in medium bowl
with the oil and chicken seasoning; mix well.
4 Lightly spray baking dish with cooking-oil
spray. Put wedges in dish. Bake, uncovered,
about 40 minutes or until wedges are
browned lightly.
5 Serve wedges with guacamole.

guacamole

Mash avocados in medium bowl; stir
in onion, tomato, juice and coriander.
(Makes 2½ cups guacamole)

per serving 34.9g total fat
(**7.1g** saturated fat); **1952kJ** (**467 cal**);
27.9g carbohydrate; **7.6g** protein; **6.3g** fibre

lemonade **ice-blocks**

ingredients:

¼ cup (60ml) lemon juice
⅔ cup (110g) icing sugar
1 cup (250ml) sparkling mineral water

method:

1 Stir juice and icing sugar in medium jug until sugar dissolves.
2 Stir in mineral water.
3 Pour mixture into four ⅓-cup (80ml) ice-block moulds. Press lids on firmly; freeze 6 hours or overnight.

per ice-block 0g total fat (**0g** saturated fat); **305kJ** (**73 cal**); **18.6g** carbohydrate; **0.1g** protein; **0g** fibre

tip

➡ **Ice-blocks are a great high-energy treat, but go easy as too much sugar can lead to tooth decay and even a loss of appetite.**
➡ **These ice-blocks can be frozen for up to a month.**

sweettreats

PREPARATION TIME 16 MINUTES (PLUS REFRIGERATION TIME) | COOKING TIME 3 MINUTES | SERVES 4

○ chocolate-dipped fruit

ingredients:

2½ cups (375g) milk chocolate Melts
2 medium bananas (400g), sliced thickly
250g strawberries
¾ cup (110g) dried apricots

method:

1 Grease oven tray; line with baking paper.
2 Place Melts in microwave-safe bowl; cook on MEDIUM-LOW (30%) in microwave oven for 1 minute. Using oven mitts, remove bowl from microwave oven; stir chocolate. If it's not completely melted, return bowl to microwave oven briefly.
3 Using hand, dip fruit, one piece at a time, into chocolate to coat about three-quarters of each piece of fruit. Place fruit, in single layer, on tray; refrigerate until set.

per serving 25.9g total fat (**15.8g** saturated fat); **2646kJ** (**633 cal**); **88.9g** carbohydrate; **11.5g** protein; **6.5g** fibre

PREPARATION TIME 20 MINUTES (PLUS REFRIGERATION TIME) | COOKING TIME 2 MINUTES | MAKES 24

○ chocolate apricot balls

ingredients:

½ cup (80g) finely chopped dried apricots
½ cup (40g) desiccated coconut
2 tablespoons condensed milk
1⅓ cups (200g) milk chocolate Melts
1 teaspoon vegetable oil

method:

1 Line oven tray with baking paper.
2 Combine apricots, coconut and condensed milk in small bowl; cover, refrigerate 15 minutes.
3 Using hands, roll level teaspoons of the apricot mixture into balls; place, in single layer, on tray. Refrigerate 15 minutes.
4 Combine Melts and oil in microwave-safe bowl; cook on MEDIUM-LOW (30%) in microwave oven for 1 minute. Using oven mitts, remove bowl from microwave oven; stir chocolate, return bowl to microwave oven. Repeat cooking and stirring until chocolate is melted.
5 Using fork, dip one ball into chocolate mixture to coat all over; place on tray. Repeat with remaining balls and chocolate mixture.

per ball 3.8g total fat (**2.5g** saturated fat); **293kJ** (**70 cal**); **7.9g** carbohydrate; **1.1g** protein; **0.6g** fibre

tip

➡ Dried apricots are a particularly good source of beta carotene, fibre and potassium.

tip

➡ When you make either of these treats, take care not to use extreme heat when melting the chocolate. And remember: only eat chocolate occasionally, and in small amounts.

PREPARATION TIME 15 MINUTES | COOKING TIME 3 MINUTES (PLUS REFRIGERATION TIME) | MAKES 54

snickers rocky road

ingredients:
4 x 60g Snickers bars, chopped coarsely
1 cup (35g) rice bubbles
150g toasted marshmallows, chopped coarsely
1 cup (140g) roasted unsalted peanuts
400g milk eating chocolate, chopped coarsely
2 teaspoons vegetable oil

method:
1 Grease 19cm x 29cm slice pan. Line base and two long sides with baking paper, extending paper 2cm above sides of pan. Combine Snickers, rice bubbles, marshmallows and nuts in large bowl.
2 Combine chocolate and oil in microwave-safe bowl; cook on MEDIUM-LOW (30%) in microwave oven for 1 minute. Using oven mitts, remove bowl from microwave oven; stir chocolate, return bowl to microwave oven. Repeat cooking and stirring until chocolate is melted; cool 5 minutes.
3 Pour chocolate mixture into Snickers mixture; mix until well combined. Spoon mixture into pan; refrigerate, covered, about 30 minutes or until set. Remove from pan, trim edges of mixture; cut into 3cm squares. Store rocky road, covered, in refrigerator.

per piece 4.3g total fat (**2g** saturated fat); **322kJ**
(**77 cal**); **8.3g** carbohydrate; **1.6g** protein; **0.5g** fibre

PREPARATION TIME 20 MINUTES | COOKING TIME 10 MINUTES (PLUS REFRIGERATION TIME) | MAKES 24

chocolate nut clusters

ingredients:
¼ cup (35g) shelled unsalted pistachios
¼ cup (35g) slivered almonds
1 cup (150g) milk chocolate Melts
½ cup (80g) sultanas

method:
1 Line oven tray with baking paper.
2 Heat small heavy-based frying pan; roast pistachios and almonds, stirring constantly, until browned lightly. (Take care; nuts burn easily.) Remove nuts from hot pan; cool.
3 Place chocolate in microwave-safe bowl; cook on MEDIUM-LOW (30%) in microwave oven for 1 minute. Using oven mitts, remove bowl from microwave oven; stir chocolate, return bowl to microwave oven. Repeat cooking and stirring until chocolate is melted.
4 Stir nuts and sultanas into chocolate.
5 Use a teaspoon to scoop out heaped spoonfuls of chocolate mixture; place onto tray. Refrigerate, uncovered, until chocolate is completely set.

per cluster 3.3g total fat (**1.2g** saturated fat); **251kJ**
(**60 cal**); **6.7g** carbohydrate; **1.2g** protein; **0.5g** fibre

PREPARATION TIME 10 MINUTES (PLUS REFRIGERATION TIME) | MAKES 24

◯ white chocolate crackles

ingredients:
1 cup (35g) rice bubbles
1 cup (35g) Coco Pops
2 x 35g tubes mini M&M's
1 cup (200g) white chocolate Melts, melted

method:
1 Line two 12-hole (1 tablespoon/20ml) mini muffin pans with patty-pan cases.
2 Combine ingredients in medium bowl. Divide mixture among prepared holes, cover; refrigerate 10 minutes.

per serving **3.3g** total fat (**2.1g** saturated fat); **293kJ** (**70 cal**); **9.3g** carbohydrate; **0.9g** protein; **0.1g** fibre

PREPARATION TIME 40 MINUTES (PLUS REFRIGERATION TIME) | COOKING TIME 5 MINUTES | MAKES 30

◯ coconut truffles

ingredients:
½ cup (125ml) coconut cream
2 teaspoons finely grated lime rind
2 teaspoons finely grated lemon rind
360g white eating chocolate, chopped coarsely
1¼ cups (85g) shredded coconut

method:
1 Combine coconut cream, rinds and chocolate in small saucepan; stir over low heat until smooth. Transfer mixture to small bowl, cover; refrigerate 3 hours or overnight.
2 Working with a quarter of the chocolate mixture at a time (keeping remainder under refrigeration), roll rounded teaspoons into balls; place on tray. Refrigerate truffles until firm.
3 Working quickly, roll truffles in coconut, return to tray; refrigerate until firm.

per truffle **6.7** total fat (**4.9g** saturated fat); **389kJ** (**93 cal**); **6.9g** carbohydrate; **1.1g** protein; **0.5g** fibre

girls'**pyjama**party

tip

➡ **Pineapple is a super fruit, full of vitamin C, healthy fibre and sweet, delicious flavour.**

PREPARATION TIME 15 MINUTES (PLUS REFRIGERATION TIME) | **MAKES** 2.5 LITRES (10 CUPS)

○ tropical punch

ingredients:
- 425g can sliced mango in natural juice
- 3 cups (750ml) tropical fruit juice
- 300g finely chopped pineapple
- 250g finely chopped strawberries
- 2 tablespoons finely shredded fresh mint
- 1 tablespoon caster sugar
- 3 cups (750ml) ginger ale

method:

1 Strain mango over small bowl; reserve juice. Chop mango slices finely.

2 Combine mango and reserved juice in large bowl with tropical fruit juice. Stir in remaining ingredients. Refrigerate punch 2 hours before serving.

156

per 250ml **0.1g** total fat (**0g** saturated fat); **422kJ** (**101 cal**); **23.6g** carbohydrate; **1.1g** protein; **1.7g** fibre

tip

➡ **Don't assemble or cook pizzas until just before serving to keep them from becoming soggy.**

PREPARATION TIME 8 MINUTES | COOKING TIME 20 MINUTES | SERVES 4

○ prosciutto and rocket pizza

ingredients:

2 x 335g pizza bases
140g pizza tomato sauce
200g provolone cheese, sliced thinly
200g thinly sliced prosciutto
100g baby rocket leaves
2 teaspoons extra virgin olive oil

method:

1 Preheat oven to hot (220°C/200°C fan-forced).
2 Place pizza bases on oven tray, top with sauce, cheese and prosciutto.
3 Bake, uncovered, about 20 minutes or until cheese has melted.
4 Serve pizzas topped with rocket and drizzled with oil.

per serving 26g total fat (**11.3g** saturated fat); **3277kJ** (**784 cal**); **93.2g** carbohydrate; **39.8g** protein; **8g** fibre

157

PREPARATION TIME 10 MINUTES (PLUS REFRIGERATION TIME) | COOKING TIME 30 MINUTES | SERVES 4

○ deep-south finger-lickin' wings

ingredients:

1kg chicken wings
2 tablespoons tomato sauce
2 tablespoons worcestershire sauce
2 tablespoons brown sugar
1 tablespoon American mustard

dipping sauce
1 tablespoon American mustard
2 tablespoons tomato sauce
1 tablespoon worcestershire sauce
2 tablespoons brown sugar

method:

1 Preheat oven to hot (220°C/200°C fan-forced).
2 Cut wings into three pieces at joints; discard tips.
Combine sauces, sugar and mustard in large bowl.
Add chicken; toss chicken to coat in marinade.
Cover; refrigerate 3 hours or overnight.

3 Place chicken, in single layer, on oiled wire rack set inside large shallow baking dish; brush remaining marinade over chicken.
4 Roast, uncovered, about 30 minutes or until chicken is well browned and cooked through. Serve chicken wings with dipping sauce.

dipping sauce
Combine ingredients in small bowl; cook, covered, in microwave oven on HIGH (100%) for 1 minute.

per serving **7.4g** total fat (**2g** saturated fat); **1229kJ** (**294 cal**); **21.2g** carbohydrate; **36g** protein; **0.8g** fibre

PREPARATION TIME 5 MINUTES | SERVES 4

○ rocky road ice-cream

ingredients: 2 x 55g Cherry Ripe bars, chopped coarsely
50g coloured mallow bakes
2 tablespoons crushed toasted peanuts
1 litre vanilla ice-cream
⅓ cup chocolate Ice Magic

method: **1** Combine Cherry Ripe, mallow bakes and
nuts in medium bowl.
2 Spoon ice-cream into four serving bowls;
drizzle ice-cream with Ice Magic then top with
Cherry Ripe mixture.

tip

➡ **Combine the chopped Cherry
Ripe and some softened vanilla
ice-cream; re-freeze then serve
scoops drizzled with Ice Magic.**

per serving 28.4g total fat (**17.7g** saturated fat);
2057kJ (492 cal); 54.9g carbohydrate;
8.2g protein; **1.7g** fibre

specialoccasions

PREPARATION TIME 20 MINUTES | COOKING TIME 30 MINUTES (PLUS COOLING TIME) | MAKES 20

Pour mixture evenly into prepared pan. **Use a cutter to cut hearts.** **Dust hearts with icing sugar.**

○ mud cake **hearts**

ingredients:

175g butter
270g dark chocolate, chopped coarsely
½ cup (110g) firmly packed brown sugar
¾ cup (180ml) water
¾ cup (110g) plain flour
¼ cup (35g) self-raising flour
1 egg
paper hearts
cocoa powder, for dusting
icing sugar, for dusting

method:

1 Preheat oven to slow (150°C/130°C fan-forced). Grease 26cm x 32cm
Swiss roll pan; line base and sides with two layers of baking paper, extending
paper 3cm above sides.
2 Place butter, chocolate, brown sugar and the water in medium saucepan.
Stir over low heat until melted. Transfer to large bowl; cool 10 minutes.
3 Add flours and egg to chocolate mixture; whisk until smooth, pour into pan.
4 Bake, uncovered, about 20 minutes; cool cake in pan.
5 Turn cake onto board; remove lining paper. Using a 5cm heart cutter, cut heart
shapes from cake. Place paper hearts in centre of cake, dust half the little cakes
with sifted cocoa and half with sifted icing sugar; carefully remove paper hearts.

per heart **11.1g** total fat (**8.6g** saturated fat); **761kJ** (**182 cal**); **18.3g** carbohydrate; **1.7g** protein; **0.9g** fibre

PREPARATION TIME 30 MINUTES | COOKING TIME 1 HOUR 10 MINUTES (PLUS COOLING TIME) | SERVES 10

○ chocolate easter cake

ingredients:

½ cup (50g) cocoa powder
½ cup (125ml) boiling water
185g butter
1½ cups (330g) firmly packed brown sugar
3 eggs
1½ cups (225g) self-raising flour
½ cup (75g) plain flour
¼ teaspoon bicarbonate of soda
¾ cup (180m) milk
2 teaspoons vanilla extract
150g small milk chocolate Easter eggs
coloured cake decorations

milk chocolate icing

400g milk eating chocolate, chopped
⅔ cup (160ml) thickened cream

method:

1 Preheat oven to moderately slow (170°C/150°C fan-forced). Grease deep 22cm-round cake pan; line base with baking paper.
2 Combine cocoa powder and the water in small bowl; whisk until smooth. Cool.
3 Beat butter and sugar in small bowl with electric mixer until light and fluffy. Add eggs, one at a time, beating until combined between additions. Transfer mixture to large bowl.
4 Stir in sifted flours and soda, then milk, extract and cocoa mixture. Pour mixture into pan.
5 Bake, uncovered, about 1 hour 10 minutes. Stand 10 minutes before turning, top-side up, onto wire rack to cool.
6 Spread milk chocolate icing over top and side of cold cake, decorate with chocolate eggs and coloured decorations.

milk chocolate icing

Combine chocolate and cream in small saucepan, stir over very low heat until smooth. Transfer to medium bowl. Refrigerate, stirring frequently, until icing is a spreadable consistency.

Mix ingredients together in a large bowl.

Pour mixture into pan, scraping out bowl with a rubber spatula.

Using a metal spatula, spread icing evenly over cake.

per serving 39.5g total fat (**24.6g** saturated fat); **3135kJ** (**750 cal**); **90g** carbohydrate; **11.7g** protein; **1.8g** fibre

PREPARATION TIME 30 MINUTES (PLUS REFRIGERATION TIME) | COOKING TIME 10 MINUTES PER TRAY | MAKES 40

Knead dough using the heel of your hand, until smooth.

Roll dough out to 4mm thick, then make into shapes using Christmas cutters.

Ice cold biscuits with tinted royal icing and decorate with cachous.

christmas gingerbread biscuits

ingredients:

125g butter, softened
½ cup (110g) firmly packed brown sugar
½ cup (125ml) treacle
1 egg yolk
2½ cups (375g) plain flour
1 tablespoon ground ginger
1 teaspoon mixed spice
1 teaspoon bicarbonate of soda
sparkling cachous

royal icing

2 egg whites
3 cups (480g) pure icing sugar
variety of food colourings

method:

1 Beat butter and sugar in small bowl with electric mixer until light and fluffy; beat in treacle and egg yolk. Transfer mixture to large bowl, stir in sifted dry ingredients. Knead dough on lightly floured surface until smooth; cover, refrigerate 1 hour.

2 Preheat oven to moderate (180°C/160°C fan-forced).

3 Roll dough between sheets of baking paper until 4mm thick. Cut shapes from dough using Christmas cutters. Make a small hole in the top of each biscuit for threading through ribbon, if desired. Place shapes 3cm apart on greased oven trays.

4 Bake, uncovered, about 10 minutes or until browned lightly (time depends on the size of the shapes). Transfer shapes to wire racks to cool. Spread or pipe royal icing onto cold biscuits; decorate with cachous.

royal icing

Beat egg whites in small bowl with electric mixer until soft peaks form. Gradually add sifted icing sugar, beat well between additions. Divide icing into several small bowls, tint each bowl of icing with colourings, as desired. Keep icing tightly covered with plastic wrap at all times to prevent it from drying out.

tip

➡ **For bold icing colours,
we used powdered food
colourings, available from
cake decorating shops
and some health food
stores. Mixing the powder
with a small amount of
hot water, before stirring
into the icing, gives a
better result; liquid
colourings can be used
for pale colours.**

➡ **Decorated gingerbread
shapes can be made two
weeks ahead; store in an
airtight container.**

per biscuit **2.8g** total fat (**1.7g** saturated fat); **523kJ**
(**125 cal**); **24.1g** carbohydrate; **1.3g** protein; **0.4g** fibre

→ **Cake can
be decorated
a day ahead;
keep frozen
until ready
to serve.**

per serving **38.9g** total fat (**25.5g** saturated fat);
2324kJ (**556 cal**); **47.1g** carbohydrate;
7.7g protein; **0.1g** fibre

PREPARATION TIME 15 MINUTES (PLUS FREEZING TIME) | SERVES 12

○ marbled ice-cream heart cake

ingredients:

4 litres neapolitan ice-cream
600ml thickened cream
¼ cup (40g) icing sugar
few drops pink food colouring
2 x 50g packets Smarties

method:

1 Take ice-cream out of freezer. Stand about 10 minutes or until just soft enough to remove from container. Using a large metal spoon, spoon ice-cream into 25cm heart-shaped cake pan (it should be big enough to hold 11 cups of liquid).

2 Cover top of ice-cream with plastic wrap. Press down on plastic until ice-cream squashes into pan and top is flat. Freeze ice-cream overnight.

3 Next day, using a tea towel (the pan will be very cold), take ice-cream out of freezer. Remove plastic wrap then run a knife around inside edge of pan. Put about 3cm of warm water in the sink and hold the pan in the water while you count slowly to five. This will melt the ice-cream a little and help the pan come off easily. Invert ice-cream cake onto serving plate, cover ice-cream loosely with plastic wrap and return to the freezer for 30 minutes.

4 Beat cream, icing sugar and a few drops of food colouring in small bowl of an electric mixer until thick.

5 Take ice-cream heart out of freezer and remove plastic wrap. Quickly spread top and side of heart with pink cream. Sprinkle with Smarties (if the ice-cream begins to melt at any time while you are decorating, put it back in the freezer to set). Return the heart to the freezer until you are ready to serve it.

When soft enough, spoon ice-cream into cake pan.

Press down on plastic until ice-cream squashes into pan and top is flat.

Spread ice-cream cake quickly with cream, then decorate.

169

PREPARATION TIME 30 MINUTES | COOKING TIME 3 HOURS (PLUS COOLING TIME) | SERVES 36

Add flours and spice to mix with apple juice.

Spread mixture evenly into prepared pan.

Level surface of cake mixture with wet metal spatula.

○ christmas cake

ingredients:

250g butter, softened
1¼ cups (275g) firmly packed brown sugar
4 eggs
2 tablespoons orange marmalade
1.5kg (7½ cups) mixed dried fruit
1½ cups (225g) plain flour
½ cup (75g) self-raising flour
2 teaspoons mixed spice
½ cup (125ml) orange juice
¼ cup (40g) blanched whole almonds

method:

1 Preheat oven to slow (150°C/130°C fan-forced). Line base and sides of deep 19cm-square cake pan with three thicknesses of baking paper, bringing paper 5cm above sides of pan.

2 Beat butter and sugar in small bowl with electric mixer until just combined. Beat in eggs, one at a time, until just combined between additions. Mixture may curdle at this point, but will come together later.

3 Scrape mixture into large bowl; add marmalade and fruit, mix thoroughly.

4 Sift flours and spice over mixture; add juice, mix well.

5 Drop dollops of mixture into corners of pan to hold baking paper in position; spread remaining mixture into pan.

6 Drop cake pan from a height of about 15cm onto bench to settle mixture into pan and to break any large air bubbles. Level surface of cake mixture with wet metal spatula; decorate top with almonds.

7 Bake, uncovered, about 3 hours. Remove cake from oven; cover pan tightly with foil; cool cake in pan.

tips

➡ Having both the butter and eggs at room temperature before you use them will help prevent the cake mixture from curdling.

➡ Cake can also be baked in a deep 22cm-round cake pan.

➡ Cover cake loosely with foil during baking if it starts to overbrown. Give the cake quarter turns several times during baking to avoid uneven browning.

➡ Covered cake in pan will go from oven to room temperature in about 24 hours. Remove cake from pan by turning cake upside down onto bench and carefully peeling lining paper away from sides but leaving base paper in place. Wrap cake tightly in plastic wrap to keep airtight, then wrap in foil. You can make the cake up to six months before you want to eat it. Store cake, in an airtight container, in the refrigerator.

➡ Leftover cake can be frozen, in an airtight container, for up to three months.

per serving **7.4g** total fat (**4.1g** saturated fat); **1016kJ** (**243 cal**); **41.6g** carbohydrate; **2.8g** protein; **2.8g** fibre

tip

➡ **Recipe can be
made a week ahead.**

per biscuit 6g total fat (**3.8g** saturated fat); **472kJ**
(**113 cal**); **14g** carbohydrate; **1.2g** protein; **0.4g** fibre

PREPARATION TIME 1 HOUR (PLUS REFRIGERATION TIME) | COOKING TIME 1 HOUR (PLUS COOLING TIME) | MAKES 36

○ stained-glass Christmas cookies

ingredients:

250g butter, softened
2 teaspoons finely grated lemon rind
½ teaspoon almond essence
¾ cup (165g) caster sugar
1 egg
1 tablespoon water
2¼ cups (335g) plain flour
90g individually wrapped sugar-free fruit drops,
    assorted colours

method:

1 Beat butter, rind, essence, sugar, egg and the water in small bowl with electric mixer until smooth (do not overbeat). Transfer to large bowl; stir in sifted flour. Knead dough on floured surface until smooth, cover with plastic wrap; refrigerate 30 minutes.
2 Preheat oven to moderate (180°C/160°C fan-forced). Line two oven trays with baking paper.

3 Using a rolling pin, gently tap the wrapped lollies to crush them slightly. Unwrap lollies; separate by colour into small bowls.
4 Roll dough between sheets of baking paper until 4mm thick. Cut shapes from dough using medium-sized cookie cutters; use very small cookie cutters to cut out the centre of each cookie to make a window. Make a small hole in the top of each biscuit for threading through ribbon, if desired.
5 Place cookies on oven trays; bake, uncovered, 5 minutes. Remove trays from oven; fill the centre of each biscuit with a few of the same-coloured lollies. Return to oven for 5 minutes or until browned lightly. Cool cookies on oven trays.

Lightly tap coloured lollies with a rolling pin to make your "glass".

Roll dough out to about 4mm thick, then cut into different shapes with biscuit cutters.

Fill cut-out centre of each biscuit with coloured lollies for a stained-glass effect.

173

PREPARATION TIME 30 MINUTES | COOKING TIME 1 HOUR (PLUS COOLING TIME) | SERVES 8

Beat mixture on medium speed until paler in colour and smooth.

Use a spatula to scrape mixture evenly into prepared pan.

Peel sides of chocolate with vegetable peeler to make curls.

chocolate birthday cake

ingredients:

125g butter, softened
1 teaspoon vanilla extract
1 cup (220g) caster sugar
2 eggs
⅔ cup (160ml) water
1⅓ cups (200g) self-raising flour
½ cup (50g) cocoa powder
white eating chocolate, for decoration
dark eating chocolate, for decoration

chocolate icing

60g butter, softened
1½ cups (240g) icing sugar
2 tablespoons cocoa powder
2 tablespoons milk

method:

1 Preheat oven to moderate (180°C/160°C fan-forced). Grease deep 20cm-round cake pan; line base with baking paper.

2 Combine butter, extract, sugar, eggs, the water and sifted flour and cocoa powder in medium bowl; beat on low speed with electric mixer until ingredients are combined.
3 Increase speed to medium; beat about 4 minutes or until mixture is smooth and paler in colour. Pour mixture into pan.
4 Bake, uncovered, about 1 hour. Stand cake in pan 5 minutes before turning, top-side up, onto a wire rack to cool.
5 Spread cold cake with chocolate icing.
6 Using vegetable peeler, peel sides of both chocolates to create curls. Sprinkle cake with chocolate curls.

chocolate icing
Beat butter in small bowl with electric mixer until light and fluffy. Gradually beat in sifted icing sugar and cocoa with the milk.

tip

➡ **Top the cake with cachous or chocolate sprinkles instead of the curls, if you prefer.**

per serving **24.6g** total fat (**15.9g** saturated fat); **2362kJ** (**565 cal**); **82.1g** carbohydrate; **6.4g** protein; **1.6g** fibre

glossary

all-bran a low-fat, high-fibre breakfast cereal based on wheat bran.

almonds flat, pointy ended nuts with pitted brown shell enclosing a creamy white kernel that is covered by a brown skin.

  blanched brown skins removed.

  flaked paper-thin slices.

  meal also known as ground almonds; nuts are powdered to a coarse flour texture for use in baking.

  slivered small pieces cut lengthways.

American-style pork ribs well-trimmed mid-loin ribs.

bacon rashers also known as slices of bacon, made from pork side, cured and smoked.

bagel small ring-shaped bread roll with a dense, chewy texture and shiny crust.

barbecue sauce a spicy, tomato-based sauce used to marinate, baste or as an accompaniment to meats.

basil we used sweet basil in our recipes, unless otherwise specified.

beef minute steak thin slices of beef topside or silverside.

beetroot also known as red beets; firm, round root vegetable.

bicarbonate of soda also known as baking soda.

breadcrumbs

  stale one- or two-day-old bread made into crumbs by grating, blending or processing.

  packaged fine-textured, crunchy, purchased white breadcrumbs.

butter use salted or unsalted (sweet) butter; 125g is equal to 1 stick butter.

buttermilk sold alongside fresh milk products in supermarkets and is commercially made by a method similar to yoghurt. Despite the implication of its name, it is low in fat and is a good substitute for dairy products such as cream or sour cream.

cabanossi a ready-to-eat sausage; also known as cabana.

cachous small, round cake-decorating sweets available in silver, gold, blue or various colours.

capers the grey-green buds of a warm climate (usually Mediterranean) shrub, sold either dried and salted or pickled in a vinegar brine; tiny young ones, called baby capers, are also available.

capsicum also known as bell pepper or, simply, pepper. They can be red, green, yellow, orange or purplish black. Seeds and membranes should be discarded before use.

cayenne pepper a thin-fleshed, long, extremely hot dried red chilli, usually purchased ground.

cheese

  bocconcini from the diminutive of boccone meaning mouthful; is the term used for baby mozzarella, a delicate, semi-soft, white cheese traditionally made in Italy from buffalo milk. Spoils rapidly so must be kept under refrigeration, in brine, for one or two days at most.

  cheddar the most common cow-milk "tasty" cheese; should be aged, hard and have a pronounced bite.

  cream cheese commonly known as Philadelphia or Philly, a soft cow-milk cheese.

  mozzarella soft, spun-curd cheese; originated in southern Italy where it is traditionally made from water buffalo milk. It has a low melting point and wonderfully elastic texture when heated, and is used to add texture rather than flavour.

  parmesan also known as parmigiano, parmesan is a hard, grainy cow-milk cheese that originated in the Parma region of Italy. The curd is salted in brine for a month before being aged for up to two years in humid conditions.

  pizza a commercial blend of varying proportions of processed grated mozzarella, cheddar and parmesan.

  provolone a mild cheese when young, similar to mozzarella. Golden yellow in colour, with a smooth shiny skin.

  ricotta soft white cow-milk cheese; roughly translates as "cooked again". It's made from whey, a by-product of other cheese making, to which fresh milk and acid are added. Ricotta is a sweet, moist cheese with a fat content of around 8.5% and a slightly grainy texture.

Cherry Ripe bar made from chocolate, coconut, sugar, cherries, glucose and milk powder.

chives related to the onion and leek; has a subtle onion flavour.

chocolate Melts discs of compound chocolate. ➡

chorizo sausage a sausage of Spanish origin, made of coarsely ground pork and highly seasoned with garlic and chillies.

cocoa powder also known as cocoa; dried, unsweetened, roasted then ground cocoa beans.

coconut

cream is obtained commercially from the first pressing of the coconut flesh alone, without the addition of water; the second pressing (less rich) is sold as the milk. Available in cans and cartons at supermarkets.

desiccated unsweetened, dried, concentrated and finely shredded coconut flesh.

shredded thin strips of dried coconut.

coriander also known as pak chee, ➡ cilantro or Chinese parsley; bright-green-leafed herb with a pungent flavour.

corn chips packaged snack food that evolved from fried corn tortilla pieces.

cornflakes crisp flakes of corn.

custard powder instant mixture used to make pouring custard; similar to North American instant pudding mixes.

custard, prepared pouring custard, available in cartons.

eggs some recipes in this book call for raw or barely cooked eggs; exercise caution if there is a salmonella problem in your area.

extract just as the word means, an extract is made by actually extracting the flavour from a food product. In the case of vanilla, pods are soaked, usually in alcohol, to capture the authentic flavour.

fillo pastry also known as phyllo; tissue-thin pastry sheets purchased chilled or frozen that are easy to work with and very versatile.

flour

plain an all-purpose flour, made from wheat.

self-raising plain flour that has been sifted with baking powder in the proportion of 1 cup plain flour to 2 teaspoons baking powder.

gelatine we used powdered gelatine; also available in sheet form known as leaf gelatine.

ginger when fresh is also known as green or root ginger; the thick gnarled root of a tropical plant. Ground ginger is used as a flavouring in cakes, pies and puddings and cannot be substituted for fresh ginger.

golden syrup a by-product of refined sugarcane; pure maple syrup or honey can be substituted.

hummus a Middle-Eastern dip made from softened dried chickpeas, garlic, lemon juice and tahini (sesame seed paste); can be purchased, ready-made, from most delicatessens, supermarkets and health food stores.

hundreds and thousands tiny sugar-syrup-coated sugar crystals that come in a variety of bright colours.

instant pudding mix a blancmange-style (sweet pudding made with milk) dessert mix.

jam also known as preserve or conserve; most often made from fruit.

kiwi fruit also known ➡ as Chinese gooseberry.

kumara Polynesian name of orange-fleshed sweet potato often confused with yam.

lamb, French-trimmed cutlet rack all the fat and gristle at the narrow end of the bone have been removed.

lavash flat, unleavened bread of Mediterranean origin.

Lebanese cucumber short, slender and thin-skinned; is also known as the European or burpless cucumber.

leek a member of the onion family; resembles the green onion but is much larger.

mallow bakes coloured marshmallow pellets; made from sugar, glucose, cornflour and gelatine.

malted milk powder instant powdered product made from cow milk and extracts of malted barley and other cereals.

maple syrup a thin syrup distilled from the sap of the maple tree. Maple-flavoured syrup or pancake syrup is not an adequate substitute for the real thing.

marmalade a preserve, usually based on citrus fruit.

mayonnaise we prefer to use whole egg mayonnaise in our recipes.

mesclun a mix of assorted young lettuce and other green leaves, including baby spinach leaves, mizuna and curly endive.

mexibeans a canned mix of red kidney beans, capsicum, tomato and spices.

glossary

mince meat also known as ground meat, as in beef, pork, lamb, veal and chicken.

mixed dried fruit a combination of sultanas, raisins, currants, mixed peel and cherries.

mixed spice a blend of ground spices usually consisting of cinnamon, allspice and nutmeg.

morello cherries also known as sour cherries. Available in jars.

muesli also known as granola, a combination of grains (mainly oats), nuts and dried fruits. Some manufacturers toast their product in oil and honey, adding crispness and kilojoules.

mushrooms, button small, cultivated white mushrooms with a mild flavour. ⬇

mustard

  dijon a pale brown, distinctively flavoured fairly mild French mustard.

  powder finely ground white (yellow) mustard seeds.

  wholegrain also known as seeded. A French-style coarse-grain mustard made from crushed mustard seeds and dijon-style French mustard.

Nutella chocolate hazelnut spread.

nutmeg the dried nut of an evergreen tree native to Indonesia; it is available in ground form or you can grate your own with a fine grater.

oil

  cooking spray we use a cholesterol-free cooking spray made from canola oil.

  olive made from ripened olives.

  extra virgin and **virgin olive oil** are the first and second press, respectively, of the olives and considered the best.

extra light or **light olive oil** is diluted and refers to taste not fat levels.

peanut pressed from ground peanuts; most commonly used oil in Asian cooking because of its high smoke point (capacity to handle high heat without burning).

sesame made from roasted, crushed white sesame seeds; a flavouring rather than a cooking medium.

vegetable oils sourced from plants rather than animal fats.

onion

  green also known as scallion or, incorrectly, shallot; an immature onion picked before the bulb has formed, having a long, bright-green edible stalk. ⬆

  red also known as red Spanish, ➡ Spanish or Bermuda onion; a large, sweet-flavoured, purple-red onion.

pancetta Italian bacon.

paprika ground dried red capsicum (bell pepper), available sweet or hot.

parsley, flat-leaf a flat-leaf variety of parsley also known as Italian parsley or continental parsley. ⬇

peanut butter peanuts ground to a paste; available as crunchy or smooth.

pide also known as Turkish bread, comes in long (about 45cm) flat loaves as well as individual rounds.

pine nuts also known as pignoli; not a nut, but a small, cream-coloured kernel from pine cones.

pistachio delicately flavoured, pale green nut with a hard shell. To peel, soak shelled nuts in boiling water for about 5 minutes; drain, then pat dry with absorbent paper. Rub skins with cloth to peel.

pitta also known as Lebanese bread. This wheat-flour pocket bread is sold in large, flat pieces that separate into two thin rounds. Also available in small thick pieces called pocket pitta.

pizza bases pre-packaged for home-made pizzas. They come in a variety of sizes (snack or family) and thicknesses (thin and crispy or thick).

plain cake crumbs made from plain uniced cake.

polenta also known as cornmeal; a flour-like cereal made of dried corn (maize), sold ground in several different textures; also the name of the dish made from it.

prawns also known as shrimp.

prosciutto cured, air-dried (unsmoked), pressed ham; usually sold thinly sliced.

puff pastry, ready-rolled packaged sheets of frozen puff pastry, available from supermarkets.

rice bubbles puffed rice product made with malt extract.

rice, long-grain elongated grains that remain separate when cooked; most popular steaming rice in Asia.

rocket also known as arugula, rugula and rucola; a peppery-tasting green leaf that can be used similarly to baby spinach leaves, eaten raw in salads or used in cooking. Baby rocket leaves are both smaller and less peppery. ➡

rolled oats also known as porridge; flattened oat grains rolled into flakes.

salami cured (air-dried) sausage heavily seasoned with garlic and spices.

salsa Spanish for sauce; a combination of tomatoes, onions, capsicums, vinegar, herbs and spices.

Snickers bar made from chocolate, peanuts, glucose, sugar, milk powder, butter and egg white.

silver beet also known as Swiss chard or chard; a leafy, dark green vegetable, related to the beet, with thick, crisp white or red stems and ribs.

soy sauce also known as sieu; is made from fermented soy beans.

spinach also known as English ⬆ spinach and, incorrectly, silver beet. Tender green leaves are good uncooked in salads or added to soups, stir-fries and stews just before serving.

stock available in cans, bottles or tetra packs. Stock cubes or powder can be used.

sugar

    brown an extremely soft, fine granulated sugar retaining molasses for its characteristic colour and flavour.

    caster also known as superfine or finely granulated table sugar.

    icing also known as confectioners' sugar or powdered sugar.

    white granulated table sugar, also known as crystal sugar. ➡

sultanas also known as golden raisins; dried seedless white grapes.

sweet chilli sauce mild, Thai sauce made from red chillies, sugar, garlic and vinegar.

sweetened condensed milk from which 60% of the water has been removed; the remaining milk is then sweetened with sugar.

taco seasoning a packaged seasoning meant to duplicate the Mexican sauce made from oregano, cumin, chillies and other spices.

Toblerone made from sugar, milk powder, cocoa, honey, almonds, glucose and egg white.

tomato

    canned whole peeled tomatoes in natural juices.

    cherry also known as tiny tim or ⬆ tom thumb tomatoes, small and round.

    egg also called plum or roma; these are smallish, oval-shaped tomatoes much used in Italian cooking or salads. ➡

    paste triple-concentrated tomato puree used to flavour soups, stews, sauces and casseroles.

    sauce also known as ketchup or catsup.

    semi-dried partially dried tomato pieces in olive oil; softer and juicer than sun-dried, but do not keep as long.

treacle thick, dark syrup not unlike molasses; a by-product of sugar refining.

veal steaks known as schnitzel.

vinegar, balsamic originally from Modena, Italy; there are now many balsamic vinegars on the market ranging in pungency and quality depending on how, and how long, they have been aged. Quality can be determined up to a point by price; use the most expensive sparingly.

wafer biscuits thin crisp biscuit generally served with ice-cream and creamy desserts; can also be layered with a sweet cream filling.

worcestershire sauce a dark-brown, thin, spicy sauce used as a seasoning for meat, gravies and cocktails and as a condiment.

yeast allow 2 teaspoons (7g) dried granulated yeast to each 15g fresh yeast.

zucchini also known as courgette.

index

index

conversion**chart**

One Australian metric measuring cup holds approximately 250ml, one Australian metric tablespoon holds 20ml, one Australian metric teaspoon holds 5ml.

The difference between one country's measuring cups and another's is within a two- or three-teaspoon variance, and will not affect your cooking results. North America, New Zealand and the United Kingdom use a 15ml tablespoon.

All cup and spoon measurements are level. The most accurate way of measuring dry ingredients is to weigh them. When measuring liquids, use a clear glass or plastic jug with the metric markings.

We use large eggs with an average weight of 60g.

dry measures

metric	imperial
15g	½oz
30g	1oz
60g	2oz
90g	3oz
125g	4oz (¼lb)
155g	5oz
185g	6oz
220g	7oz
250g	8oz (½lb)
280g	9oz
315g	10oz
345g	11oz
375g	12oz (¾lb)
410g	13oz
440g	14oz
470g	15oz
500g	16oz (1lb)
750g	24oz (1½lb)
1kg	32oz (2lb)

liquid measures

metric	imperial
30ml	1 fluid oz
60ml	2 fluid oz
100ml	3 fluid oz
125ml	4 fluid oz
150ml	5 fluid oz (¼ pint/1 gill)
190ml	6 fluid oz
250ml	8 fluid oz
300ml	10 fluid oz (½ pint)
500ml	16 fluid oz
600ml	20 fluid oz (1 pint)
1000ml (1 litre)	1¾ pints

length measures

metric	imperial
3mm	⅛in
6mm	¼in
1cm	½in
2cm	¾in
2.5cm	1in
5cm	2in
6cm	2½in
8cm	3in
10cm	4in
13cm	5in
15cm	6in
18cm	7in
20cm	8in
23cm	9in
25cm	10in
28cm	11in
30cm	12in (1ft)

oven temperatures

These oven temperatures are only a guide for conventional ovens.
For fan-forced ovens, check the manufacturer's manual.

Mark	°C (Celsius)	°F (Fahrenheit)	Gas
Very slow	120	250	½
Slow	150	275-300	1-2
Moderately slow	170	325	3
Moderate	180	350-375	4-5
Moderately hot	200	400	6
Hot	220	425-450	7-8
Very hot	240	475	9

Senior editor Wendy Bryant
Designer Anna Lazar
Food director Pamela Clark
Food editor Louise Patniotis
Special feature photographer Tanya Zouev
Special feature stylist Christine Rooke
Special feature food preparation Angela Muscat

ACP Books
Editorial director Susan Tomnay
Creative director Hieu Chi Nguyen
Editorial coordinator Jaime Lee
Director of sales Brian Cearnes
Marketing director Matt Dominello
Marketing manager Bridget Cody
Production manager Cedric Taylor
Chief executive officer John Alexander
Group publisher Pat Ingram
General manager Christine Whiston
Editorial director (WW) Deborah Thomas
WW food team Lyndey Milan, Alexandra Elliott, Frances Abdallaoui

Produced by ACP Books, Sydney.
Printed by Tien Wah Press (Pte) Limited, 4 Pandan Crescent, Singapore 128475.
Published by ACP Publishing Pty Limited,
54 Park St, Sydney; GPO Box 4088, Sydney, NSW 1028.
Ph: (02) 9282 8618 Fax: (02) 9267 9438
www.acpbooks.com.au
acpbooks@acpmagazines.com.au
To order books phone 136 116 (within Australia)
Send recipe enquiries to reccipeenquiries@acpmagazines.com.au

RIGHTS ENQUIRIES
Laura Bamford, Director ACP Books
lbamford@acpmedia.co.uk

AUSTRALIA: Distributed by Network Services,
GPO Box 4088, Sydney, NSW 1028.
Ph: (02) 9282 8777 Fax: (02) 9264 3278.
UNITED KINGDOM: Distributed by Australian Consolidated Press (UK),
Moulton Park Business Centre, Red House Rd, Moulton Park, Northampton, NN3 6AQ
Ph: (01604) 497 531 Fax: (01604) 497 533 books@acpmedia.co.uk
CANADA: Distributed by Whitecap Books Ltd, 351 Lynn Ave,
North Vancouver, BC, V7J 2C4 Ph: (604) 980 9852 Fax: (604) 980 8197
customerservice@whitecap.ca www.whitecap.ca
NEW ZEALAND: Southern Publishers Group,
44 New North Road, Eden Terrace, Auckland.
Ph: (64 9) 309 6930 Fax: (64 9) 309 6170 hub@spg.co.nz
SOUTH AFRICA: Distributed by PSD Promotions (Pty) Ltd,
PO Box 1175, Isando, 1600, Gauteng, Johannesburg, SA.
Ph: (011) 392 6065 Fax: (011) 392 6079 orders@psdprom.co.za

Clark, Pamela.
The Australian Women's Weekly Kids In The Kitchen
Includes index.
ISBN-13 978 1 86396 518 7
ISBN-10 1 86396 518 1
1. Cookery – Juvenile literature.
I. Title. II Title: Australian Women's Weekly.
641.5123
© ACP Publishing Pty Limited 2006
ABN 18 053 273 546

Cover Cheese, corn and bacon muffins, page 34
Photographer Tanya Zouev
Food preparation Angela Muscat

Photographers Alan Benson, Steve Brown, Gerry Colley, Joshua Dasey,
Ben Dearnley, Joe Filshie, Louise Lister, Andre Martin, Prue Ruscoe,
Brett Stevens, Ian Wallace, Andrew Young
Stylists Wendy Berecry, Julz Beresford, Janelle Bloom, Kate Brown,
Marie-Helene Clauzon, Georgina Dolling, Kay Francis, Jane Hann,
Amber Keller, Michaela le Compte, Michelle Noerianto, Sarah O'Brien

The publishers would like to thank Queen Bee Balloon and Party Shop for
props used in photography.